Lazybones:

The war in my mind

—madalyn

Lazybones: the war in my mind

To request permission, contact
lazybones.thewarinmymind@gmail.com

First paperback edition April 2024

Cover design by madalyn and the artist fat hog

ISBN 979-8-218-37438-9 (paperback)

Published by Madalyn Vaquero

To my parents, who have supported me through all my crazy endeavors, and to the Helper, who teaches me all things— Thank you.

John 14:26

Out of a season of deep ache and perpetual sin,
to a season of what I thought was blatant laziness,
I began to write; there came change, productivity, and growth,
but most importantly, I learned to trust, love, and live for Christ.
And I began to understand that time spent seeking Him
is never wasted time, regardless of how this foolish world
chooses to see it; I'm now learning to see everything
through the eyes of faith.

Contents

—

Lazybones: The war in my mind

The Almond Tree

Darling, remember Him
When your hair turns white
Like a blooming almond tree.

When your skin wrinkles with
Every slight movement—

And all the light around you
Turns ever so dim.

When your bones ache from
Old age and restless sleep.

When the sound of chirping birds
Is a tender but faint melody.

Darling, please remember Him
While you are young—

And the rain coated streets
Glisten with a future
Of endless possibilities.

The lemon tree I never had

This is the kind of love I have
For someone who will never
Love me back.

My weeping
Brings my garden back to life—

I wish it could die,
But it blooms louder
Till it becomes sour,
And I lose all sense of time.

Except for tonight,
I miss you way too much

12:16am
2:07am
3:54am
4:23am

Sleep escapes my mind,
My heart can't handle
The thought of never having you
In my life.

Do you remember
When you promised me
A beautiful garden?

And I said, *a lemon tree*
Will be the first thing I plant.

That summer, yellow surrounded me.
Now, it's a grey winter all year long.

You know that I hate the cold,
And you know how hard it is
To tend a garden—

Especially when it's freezing
In my mind.

Oh, how I dreamt of
Growing old with you,
Forever being in love with you,
Keeping our garden alive.

Now, it's all mine—
Alluring and fruitful,
Till I'm reminded of the thing
I never had,
For you were never mine
To keep.

The cactus

Questions of growing
And what is patience
And how do I practice love,
How long does it take a seed to germinate;
How long till my time comes?

I wait next to the window,
My tears dry up in the sun—
Father, some say I'm hard to love.
My prickly surface keeps them away,
But what if I want them to be my friends?

I'm tired of being lonely;
I don't like feeling this way.
I'm so small, timid, at times afraid—

I get called insignificant in this giant world
Surrounded by trees so big
That topple with one gust of wind.

I guess their roots were not that deep,
And that's the difference between
Them and me.

And even though I've been seen as shallow,
And my words I prefer to swallow—
I know that's not who I am.

But the world likes to crush me
Because I'm a little different, a little weird—
This tiny, lonely, prickly, quiet thing.

And I'm aware that I can't force others
To see me differently,
But I can choose to love them
Regardless of what they think of me.

Somnolence

Have you ever wandered
Why the moon lingers
On your darkest nights

How erratic is the sky
One hour, it's dark
The next, it's bright

Between you and me
We could stay up all night
And count the stars

Breathe in the familiarity of
What it was like to have
An unhinged mind

But darling,
You have nothing
To worry about;
I've only whispered
Your secrets to the sun

For June

I became everything you wanted me to be,
Of course, it was all for you and not for me.
So what do I do with this brokenness you left?
You promised forever would be our quest.
Now, all the places you said we would see
Are left unexplored and empty.
You tried to turn my heart of glass into stone,
I still feel the pain deep in my bones,
But I forgive you for all you've done
Because I know how it feels to be forced to run—
To try to escape a past so cruel and dark
And hide the gruesome marks
Left by someone who didn't care at all.
I just wish you hadn't made me feel so small—
The love I had for you always made me think
That no storm could ever make our boat sink.
And I understand the heartache of your past,
But a shadow on me you didn't have to cast.
I hope time heals your open wounds
And reminds you of our lovely June
Spent together sipping lemonade—
Please know, I don't see you as a renegade.

And although I'm hurt and my heart you did shake,
I promise to never again make this mistake;
To be everything someone wants me to be,
For I know I should be unashamed and free
To be who Christ has called me to be completely,
And be loved deeply—
Not just for June,
But until the sun becomes the moon.
For all of my days,
I wish to be loved by a piercing embrace.
I say this standing face to face,
The reflection on the mirror my fingers can trace.
She has hurt me so badly because I know
She's aching herself, but now she wants to grow
And promises to let go
Of everything that's dimming her glow.
For June was just a small glimpse
Of a future already foretold.

The vagabond

And she said,
Time flies,
But when will I
Get my wings
To give my feet a rest
And my heart, a test.

Will I fly above the trees,
Will I think I'm better
Than those traveling by car,
For wings could take me far
In mere seconds.

It seems I'm a wanderer
By choice—
I have no home.
Here on earth, I feel like
I don't belong,
And I think I never will.

My feet are set to sail,
My soul as free as the wind,
I go wherever, whenever,
My mind fully at peace,
My heart at ease.

Two years later...

I now recognize that
I did have duties,
I did have cares—
What I didn't have was
Genuine freedom and peace.
But I've now met full freedom,
If you're interested—
I can show you where.

On my knees,
In His word,
I'm grounded in my steps
So that I may be humble in the air.

Following with poise,
Tuning out the noise,
His gentle care
Leading me to where I belong.
Like the clouds, like ever-flowing rivers,
I'm relentless in His presence
Or still when He needs me to be.

I rest in His palm, sit at His feet,
I go wherever He tells me,
Whenever He tells me,
And like a bird of passage,
I've wandered—
But I now know I'll never
Be lost again.

A

When you drew a heart on my hand,
I think that was the last time I saw you.
I whispered our friendship goodbye,
Missed you till I went mad,
How could I have done you so wrong?
But can you please try to understand,
The anxiety was killing me
So I had to do what I do best,
I had to get up and leave,
Go away to breathe some fresh air.
A second, at most,
That's the time I spent
To repair the clock
And go back to a time
When we weren't yet friends.

Bones

Pound per pound
Breath × ten
She knew if she stepped off
The numbers would disappear
But she stood there—
The weight of the world
Crushing her very last bone

I wish she would've been told
A story of love
Instead of being torn apart
By her own thoughts
And by those who judge
With just a glance

Roots

Like mermaids, we swam all day
Till our skin disappeared.
Searched for all the wonders
Of the world and fell in love
With the small things—
The simplicity of breath in my lungs,
The complexity in thinking my exhale is
Destroying our earth to the core.
My small treasure, my almost nothing;
The tiny white house on the hill—
Contemplating if I'll settle in a lonely place
Where nature outgrows its space.
You know, crowded never suited me well.
Finally, my roots are starting to show—
I've decided I'm okay with that.
There's no need to change,
There's no need to compromise
My precious childhood nest—
Even if people choose to
Love me any less.

Open Flame

Why do you want to be like everyone else?
Yeah, it's true,
We're all more alike than different—
Clay sculpted by the Sculptor,
Shining all the same.
Within, a delicately placed ceramic,
Inimitable in its color.
Put through fire,
Shaped and maybe with time, chipped—
Yet still as beautiful in its own way.
Its smooth curves, its rough surface,
The way it wilts
When an open flame
Gently caresses its skin,
A whisper crackling
Through every pocket of air
Ready to burst at any moment.
It's who we are, right?
Or are you going to tell me you've never
Licked your finger and tried to tame the flame?
Never lied, or pretended that you're okay?
Tell me, why do you think
You're different from everyone else?

The Jungle

Soft silent fears
Falling gently like
The leaves on a tree,
With her head held high,
Her bosom cradling a baby
With a baleful look of despise.

"How could you be so blind?
Fostering the hope of someone
Whose soul has already died
In the jungle where you get
Trampled to death,
Not by misfortune,
But by those who
Boast in vain."

Hard thunderous tears
Fell dangerously like trees
In a storm, hastily tumbling down,
As she looked at her
Empty hands and bare chest,
All hope now gone.

"The child—
Well, he's no longer a child,
Turned out to be exactly like those
You see in the movies—
The ones that disturb your sleep
And infiltrate your dreams,
Now I only know of nightmares."

All the words I've never said

They gave me their ears
And I wasted away.
All my energy,
All the words I've never said.
It feels like no one truly listens—
Except when there's self-gain.
We pretend to care,
When in reality,
We're locked in our own world.
There are times I wish
I would've never opened my mouth
To tell them the things
No one else knows about.
Thinking they'd understand—
Oh the many endeavors
To help a grieving world,
But I've shut down;
I don't want to be a part of humanity—
Anymore.

Can one grain of salt
Really make a change?
Does it matter if I hate myself
Even more than I hate everyone else?

Mars

The thing is, that's not quite true
(The part about hating myself and others)
At least not anymore.
I'm learning to understand,
I'm learning to love again.
I just—sometimes wish
I could go to mars, build a tiny house
And have it all to myself.
I know it sounds selfish,
I know it can come across as narcissistic,
But I'm sick to the very bone of feeling this way—
Like I give and give, and others just take away.
No one ever stops to ask me—how's my day.
Hours upon hours,
My eardrums are going to burst.
You may ask, who has hurt you so badly?
Surely, it cannot be the whole world?
And to that I answer—
Surely not, I've seen a lot of kindness,
I've experienced so much compassion;
I felt the tender love of the lady
Who smiled at me last week,
A smile like no other—
It's been a while, since I see one
So genuine, truly placid—
The kind I long to have, one that not even
The scariest of nightmares can shake away.

M.A.R.S

I'm sick and I'm tired
Of showing that I care,
Of trying to understand,
I'm not saying that makes me any better—

Maybe I'm all the worst for it.
And maybe others feel the same way, but as of now,
Reasonable doubts fill my mind as to why
Sleep might be the only friend I'll ever have.

**When did you know
That I loved you?**

B's pov

Was it when I told you to close your eyes
And count to ten?
Was it when I showed up at your doorstep
With sunflowers?
Was it when I sang your favorite song as
You counted all the green cars that drove by?
Was it when I drew a picture of your silly cat
And then mailed it to you?
Was it when I giggled because you spilled
The orange juice all over yourself?
Was it when we watched Breakfast at Tiffany's
And I held you in my arms?
You cried for an hour because Cat,
The poor slob without a name,
Reminded you of your childhood cat.
Was it when I learned all the lyrics to your
Favorite musical just so that I could sing along?
Was it the night I tried to bake cookies and
They turned into little black rocks?
Was it when we spent hours in an empty parking lot
Talking nonsense till dusk became dawn?

Or
Was it when I finally said the words, *I love you*,
And you couldn't say them back,
So you ran out the door
And left my heart in pieces,
But the worst thing of all is
That you never came back.
I think you should know that
My heart is still shattered beyond repair,
And every waking moment
My mind spins the same question;
Did you ever love me, even for just a second?

Wide World

We were quarantined in our mind,
Wanted a freedom we never really had,
We were desperate to run back to
What we thought was normal, but normal
Was just familiarity in disguise, tell me,
Would you ever go back to a time
When you had a depressed mind,
When anxiety ran high, or
Would you rather step into a future
Where you can have freedom and never
Walk backward to a comfort that
Was nothing but a demise?

Golden Sunflower

The earth is getting hotter,
But You've always known this—
And some fear the end is near,
But there's still time to heal.
Time no longer makes sense to me,
And I almost feel like I don't fear a thing.
I stand tall and joyful amongst the
Sunflowers in the field,
As golden as I'll ever be,
For old age is coming and I don't know
If it'll be kind to me or strip me of everything.
So I gather all that means well to me,
And in the holy ground, I let my roots grow deep.
There, I patiently wait for my love to steep,
For there's a task You've left for me—
Just like wildfires spread from tree to tree,
I hope to spread Your word,
Planting seed by seed,
For the need is great, and the end is near.

Behind Closed Doors

Who are you behind closed doors,
When no one is watching,
In the places only you know?
Do your knees tremble?
Do your lips quiver?
Your semblance, tell me,
How long did it take to achieve it?
I'm not here to judge,
I'm just here to listen.
Perhaps there's a heaviness
You've been carrying,
Things you would never want
The world to know,
But you can let me know.

I noticed
You have a new face,
Plastered—
Trying to hide your grimace,
But no one is watching,
You don't have to pretend
That everything's fine and you're okay.
I know you're
Wallowing in the darkness,
Drowning in your sorrows—
Your pain I see and share,
But I need you to listen;
There is One who can tear your walls down
And free you from the pit of despair.

That way, you'll hear the truth clearly
And hold it dearly—
Hoping one day you'll call me
A friend again,
Even more so, hoping you come to know
The God Almighty who reigns,
For only then can one acknowledge
The gifts He gives—
Of peace, joy, and an endless love
Where you don't have to keep up
With the trends of this world.

Tell me, why do you feel the pressure
To keep the cameras rolling
Behind the curtains?
Why do you feel so defenseless?
Why are you acting like you're
Alone and completely helpless?
He doesn't even need you to meet Him
Halfway; He already did what we
Couldn't do ourselves.
For He has never and will never
Forsake His children,
And He hears our every word—

Really,
Every shout, cry, mumbled phrase—
Everything, He has heard.
Friend, I just wish you would say it
All to my face, nothing will ever
Be too deranged.
For I, too, am imperfect—
Full of flaws everywhere.

So, who are you behind closed doors,
When no one is watching,
When you're truly alone?
The truth is,
He has always known,
But are you willing to find out?
Are you weary, heavy-laden, full of doubt?

If so, I urge you to come to Him,
For He is the only One who can
Heal your brokenness,
Restore your collapsed mind,
And lead you to a life in the light—
One where you won't feel
The need to hide,
And all your selfish pride
Will vanish along with your walls
Because you don't need a
False security
In the realm of His love.

And know that your desires
Will completely change;
Your life will completely change—
For we are called to be holy
Like our God,
Not at war, but at peace,
Not in secrecy, but in unity,
Without walls, doors, and curtains.
Let His light shine through you,
And know that all I want
For you is good.
So friend, will you please
Stop ignoring my texts and calls—
You've left me in exile for far too long.

Wisdom

On her right hand
She offers you a prolonged life,
On her left—
Treasures and dignity,
As she guides you
Down her graceful path—
All her rivers, alive and abundant.

My Father's daughter

The anxiety tingling in her fingertips,
Making its way to her scalp.
What keeps her sane or is she going insane?
Day after day—the battle drags on,
Taking her piece by piece,
As if old age hasn't been greedy enough.

I think back to yesterday, I think of tomorrow
And the years to come—
But then I think about her childhood
And what her dreams must've been like;
Were they a forest or an open field?
Do they even matter to her anymore
Or has she lost every strand of hope?

I often wonder if I could handle walking in her life,
For her shoes are just my size.
But when I ponder a little longer, I become immediately
Aware that her burden would instantly crush me;
Oh Lord, now I'm able to understand that she endures
Because of Your unfailing love.

I can't imagine what it must've been like
To be surrounded by violent wars,
To hear and fear gunshots, to watch her father die—
Killed by his best friend on a drunken night.
Merely a child, but already working from dawn to dusk.

Did she ever get to play with toys?
Laugh with all the girls and boys?
Was labor the only thing she knew?
I often wonder, when was the exact
Moment she met You?

So many years have gone by,
Yet I can't tell if it feels like
An eternity or a blink of an eye.
All I know is that for her,
It certainly feels like a lifetime.

When will she finally get to run into her mother's arms,
Before Time comes to steal
The last shred of her mother's mind?
Oh Lord, how long must she keep waiting
For this day to come?

Their precious memories are slowly fading
Away like the morning fog.
Her tear-filled days, her lonely nights
Covered in bog; she's sinking,
She's heartbroken and mystified—
Thinking of all the tunes her mother used to sing
As she tucked her into bed at night.
Years and years of quietly humming them,
Now they're just an echo
Bouncing on the empty walls of her scattered mind.
Oh Lord, how her ears crave their sound.
How I long to see her smile and not frown.
Father, please tell me, will she ever be the jolly
Old soul I used to know?

———

Will she at least get to hear her mother's voice
One final time, face to face,
No longer through a phone?
Will she get one last embrace, before time breaks
Her mother's brittle bones?
Oh Lord, I don't know about her,
But I'm still full of hope.

So Father, Your daughters are pleading,
Will You please answer our prayer?
Grant her this one thing
That I so desperately wish for,
That she seems to desperately need;
May she get to see her mother
Before old age comes and goes,
Before both of their minds are completely gone.

We know that You can make it happen,
But it won't happen if it's not Your will—
And what we ultimately want is for Your will to be done.
Therefore, we pray in faith,
Knowing that we rest in Your embrace,
No matter the outcome; no matter how this story ends.

We'll patiently wait for an answer—
A no or a yes.
Or perhaps there will be silence, and we'll learn
To trust You even more through it.
But one thing I'm sure of—no matter what,
We're no longer orphans; You're our Father,
Our merciful providence, our home.

So thank You, for although we now suffer,
We know that it is only temporary because Your Son
Bore our sin and shame; we'll see You face to face
On that very day, but even now, Your Spirit is with us
Through our hills and through our bends.
So in the valley of the shadow of darkness, Your light
Will lead Your sons and daughters to the heavenly realm,
Where there will be no more longing and pain,
Where Your daughter won't groan about earthly matters
Because she will see the glory of her Father,
Who is teaching her to trust in His promises
And to understand why things must happen a certain way,
And how His purpose will always prevail,
For His thoughts and ways are higher than what any
Fallible human mind could ever comprehend.

Monsters and Men

Let them lie face down
On the crystalline ground,
Finally understanding what it means to be alive.
May there be hope
One day, somehow,
For the wicked, the lonely and
The abundantly loved.

Who's to say they are different?
And who's to say monsters only come out at night?
I've seen men in the shadows
Doing wrong,
But nobody stopped to tell them
What it was that they were doing wrong.
So they kept living, flesh fully attached.

Yet I've seen monsters being
Taunted and tossed,
Constantly getting made fun of,
And being told that they will never be loved.
I've tried to judge them, but I found myself
Sitting, listening—compelled by their
Heartbreaking stories and the agony of their past.

To me, a monster is anyone who seeks to do wrong,
Who makes fun of others and wishes to destroy lives,
So where do we draw the line?

I'm sure I've been a monster to some
And a human to others.
And ugly creature, a pretty face,
But what is beauty?
And what is beauty from the heart?

I grow tired of thinking, of sitting,
So I lie down on the crystalline ground,
And I hope,
And I love,
With the knowledge that tomorrow
I may see the sun rise again—
Oh, how lucky I am
To be alive.

Cage

My heart, a stone
That dissolves
But forms back again.
In my throat, a wound
That I pick at,
Yet wonder why it
Never seems to heal.
And my feet cannot
Stay still,
So my mind starts
To wonder
What it would feel like
To be in love.
As the light turns green,
My heart skips a beat
And turns to stone
Once again.
And my throat is bleeding
From all the songs
I've locked in a cage.
But how do I set them free?
How can I put an end to
All the madness?
How does one turn a heart
Of stone into a heart of flesh?

Talk to me

Dear friend, please talk to me.
How are you?
How's your heart? Does it bleed purple?
Does it ache?
Tell me,
How do you keep the peace?
Because my flesh wants to
Set on fire everything that's in its way.
You know, I don't want to continue
Being the same—
And just watch myself decay.

But my spirit,
My spirit doesn't know what to do.
It hurts it breaks
It crawls lowly it withers away—
To see those who kill for desire
Light a fire, their eyes glimmering
As the flames destroy everything
In their way—
It boils the blood through my veins.
So how do I educate with love and mercy?
How do I stop the hurricane
From reaching the bay?
How do I kneel without hating
Those who oppress?
How do I continue helping
Without growing tired or depressed?
How do I seek God and forgo the world?

Tell me,
Is there an even greater pain?
Because it feels like
We once danced in perfect circles,
Now we're bent out of shape.
And so I pray,
If it be my Father's will,
For a change to come,
For His children to stand
Hand in hand
Till the end
Because He created us all the same.
Precious—
Is every color of skin
That keeps our sack of bones
Safely inside
Whilst we wait for our final day,
Knowing that His children have
Been spared from a wrath so great,
So powerful, terrifying, just,
And of course, holy.

The panic and the flame

Life spins and spins—
I draw endless circles,
And I don't know
How to stop,
How to stand still,
How to breathe,
When to rest,
I live in the constant test.

It sends my mind into overdrive.
I don't want to freeze
So I overreact—
And that's when
The manic begins.

The panic and the flame
Inflict pain
And encircle my body—
But I don't like the cold
So I let it burn.

Now everything of mine
Is ashes,
And like a Phoenix,
I need to be born again—

—

And again and again.
Vicious circles that
I loathe yet can't seem to end.

One would think that by now
I would be pretty good
At drawing perfect circles,
But they just keep getting
Worse and worse.

So if this will be my endless cycle,
Can I at least scatter my ashes
In my favorite place?
And watch myself bloom
Into an enchanting garden—
Hoping that one day
I'll live forever
And never burn.

Unlike here,
In my heart, in my brain—
Unlike earth; where the panic
Begets the flame
And the flame induces the panic
Then it all leads to madness—
So where does the circle begin and end?

1st Vineyard

The vines of entanglement, it seems no one can escape;
They wrap around bodies like the mind grapples with death—

Their limbs cannot handle anymore tears,
Their bodies can no longer withstand the distress,
Their minds echo, keep fighting just a little longer,
As the vines pull apart bone and flesh—

I tried to help, but they refused it,
They told me it would make them look weak,
Like a frail dog starving on the streets—

So now I just sit and weep,
Watching the sunset from my vineyard,
But no matter how rich my harvest,
My heart returns to the tangled mess—

The blood, the bruises, the harrowing screams,
Where there once was a scar, now a gaping wound
Flows endlessly, like a stream—

And time passes me by, but my mind
Is still being haunted by the wicked vines—

I am a river of tears, I am an awful friend,
Did I do enough to help?

Alone does not mean lonely

Don't mistake my one for pain,
I much prefer it this way.
In a crowded place, I tend to feel the loneliest,
So I'd rather keep my distance—
It makes it difficult to find a lover,
A real one that won't run away
When things get hard and the world decides
To scream out loud all the things you hate about yourself.

That doesn't mean I don't love people or myself,
But it's hard to turn a blind eye
To all the pain we inflict upon ourselves and others,
To all the trashing of the earth,
To all the kinds of evil found in this world.
It breaks me, dissolves me into
Another realm, a void I cannot explain,
An empire of burnt remains,
Where I rummage to find the broken
And give the pieces a new name.

You know, for the longest time,
I wanted to change my name
To one that's less inviting, I suppose,
To keep others away.
That's how much I enjoy
My own company, a journey
Some find hard to take,
But I'm finding it harder to tell
Others to come and stay.

Runaway

If the home in my heart is haunted,
Where does my soul go?
If I live out of fear and not love,
Who does my soul owe?

For my soul was gobsmacked
By the hypocrisy in religion—
Until I received my eyesight
And learned to hang tight
So that I would not be afraid to fly.

For what You've given me
Cannot be taken away by mortal, immoral men.
If Your Spirit is with me,
There's no need to run away—

Yet I've traveled these roads all my life;
When will the haunting ever stop?
I run in the discomfort, the frustration, the pain,
The dark thoughts inside my brain.
I'm sick, I'm tired, sometimes—
I'm terrified of fear itself.

But if fear is pain and pain is gain
Then what is love?
If love is God and God is love
Then who am I?

Most certainly—
Not a child of wrath, for I now abide in Him;
I have a home, and I'm learning to glorify Him
With my life.

—

Pure Bliss

She said,
"How honest do you
Want me to be tonight?"
I said, "brutally honest,
Like the I wanna cry
Myself to sleep type—
Whether it's from
Heartache or pure bliss,
I just need to know
What's on your mind."
So she told me everything
I had done wrong,
And that's when I knew
I had found a gem;
An everlasting friend.

Oh daughter

Stop ripping your hair out,
Stop picking at your skin.
I just wish it were as easy
As telling you to stop,
But it's not—
You can't help it,
You keep digging and digging,
Pulling and pulling
Till it bleeds,
And the wounds never seem to heal.
It tears me apart.
It's hard for me to watch.
It feels like you're fading away—
I just wish it were as easy
As telling you to stop.
You seem anxious and depressed,
But I don't know what more to do to help.
Please know that you're still
A great mother and a great daughter,
And I will always see you as a close friend,
No matter how much you pull—
No matter how much it feels like
You're pushing me away.
It absolutely wrecks me
To see you in this state.

I feel like a failure
Because I don't know how to help.
But I look to a future
Where you will be healed and safe,
At peace with everything—
Holding your child's hand.
Please know, it pains me that we're estranged,
Like distant family you see
Here and there.
Or even worse—
Two strangers who just met
And their social anxiety
Won't let them communicate.
I don't know what to say.
I'm hurting
Because you're hurt,
And you can't seem to stop hurting yourself.
I've ran out of things to do for you to let me in,
It becomes harder and harder
With every drop of blood,
With every strand of hair on the ground,
With every teardrop that falls from your eyes.
I think I'll probably lose my mind
Before you're done pulling all your hair out,
Or perhaps my Heavenly Father will mend
Your broken heart just in time—

And He did.

Under my bed

There's a big mess
Under the place
I lay to rest
Broken dreams
Unsung melodies
Pages filled with
Nonsensical things
Suppressed memories
Lost hope
Loves forgotten
Crushed projects
Unfulfilled promises
Empty boxes
Dusty shoes
Things that remind me
Of heartache
Things that remind me
Of You
And so much more
Is stuffed
Under my bed

There's a big mess
Born out of my mind
Oh my silly little mind
You are getting too crowded
But now it's time for me to be brave
Dig through the mess
And decide what I need
To let go of and
What still needs to be shared
I can't keep hiding
Everything under my bed
Just because I'm afraid
Of the world judging me
Leaving me cold and bare
Oh Lord how I hate feeling like
The talents You have given me
Will never be enough
But I need to believe
In You not in me
Because You created me
And gave me such things
So that I may praise
Your mighty name for all eternity
For by learning to place my trust in You
I know there will no longer be
Anything under that is unfit
Because You are showing me
True rest proper sleep
And how to bring into the light
All that's hidden deep within me
So that I may praise You Lord
With everything

Flies

Precious things, you don't let them mold,
I've seen her piling and piling for so long.
She must be so tired from
Carrying such a heavy load.
I can't imagine what she has gone through,
What stream of tears she has
Accumulated through the years—
Physically, she's awake,
Mentally, she's an unconscious mess—
Senseless, worthless, loveless,
The lies her brain says to her face.

Nation Divided   11/19

The nation is divided.
There are millions of little pieces
Roaming around—

And you can't speak the truth
Without being told you are wrong.

But I'm learning to see things
From a heavenly perspective;
It differs from the rest of the world.

It can feel isolating at times,
An alien-like otherworldliness of loneliness,
Although I imagine there are others
Who also feel this way, so I find comfort
In the silence, for I know that I'm not alone;
We're not alone.

On the periphery of the bustling towns
There's always an island,
That's where I usually spend my time now—

Yet as I walk on these oh-so-common streets,
I can't help but feel the ache and despair
Of those who long for a true friend—
Like I once did.

Hearts break, truth hurts, beauty fades,
It's all booze, drugs, and silly games—

We live like irresponsible adults
Stuck in a four-year-old's brain.

And in my vicinity,
I can see the millions of little pieces
Raising their fists while screaming,
"Who said we must grow up?
Can't we be the kids who never grow old?"

...

What a friend I've found

Yeah,
> But innocence has left

So we think we're stuck being
The people pleasers
The can't say no
The ones who cast the first stone
The ones who don't care at all.
The left is right and the left is wrong
The ones who write about subjects
That some say can't be touched—

We swallow copious amounts
Of pills to suppress pain
Paint on faces with a different name
Starve to fit into a venomous frame
Let the media mold us until we go insane
Laugh at someone's mistakes
Yet get mad when they do that to our face
Misjudge those who ask for help
Then wonder why they pulled the trigger
On themselves
Live in the valley of regret
Pondering the things we can't forget—

That was my home for so long,
But what a friend I've found in
Jesus.

Resolutions

To not be in a hurry
To not worry
To know that I'm Yours

Lavender Skies

She wondered if her voice would ever only be an echo,
If her feet could ever be untied and set to twirl.
As swift as a thud of thunder, the darkest dark set upon her,
And her lavender skies soon began to swirl
Into a ubiquitous image she couldn't quite shake.
The abounding clouds began to dance
To a tune of an unspeakable fate,
And in her mind, a drought that only brought about
Thoughts of guilt and shame,
Wishing she could start over with a clean slate.
She felt the tears walking down her face, reminding her
Of how lucky she was to have seen the autumn rain.
But with her skies now the deepest shade of grey,
Came a sense of longing and an unbearable pain;
A desire to escape her "fate" and paint her skies
With the loveliest pastels.
Yet little did she know, she was destined to live
Cradled by love and peace,
In this mad world that shakes without relent,
Where the crushing of the mind never seems to cease—
Soon, she'll look around
And recognize everything in her life for what it is—
a masterpiece.

Plastic Thoughts

I was living
One step forward,
One step back,
Tired of wondering,
Yet not ever moving at all.

My love for You was fragile,
Somehow it withstood
The test of time—

In these great new depths,
You brought me to explore
The caverns of my heart,
Set fire to the reckless homes
In my mind,
And then rebuilt them—
Refurnished them
With lustrous thoughts.

All the while saying to myself,
What a painstaking process—
You took my shame,
Wrapped it up,
Then threw it in the waves.
Unlike plastic,
Everything I did and said,
In one second—
I saw it disintegrate.

Oh, what a wondrous surprise;
You use our very pain
To clothe us in an armor
Stronger than any weapon
Forged through fire,
So as the battle against
Earthly desires continues,
We persevere on and on,
For Your word sustains us
Through the storms of life—
There, no flame of sin
Will ever survive.

So no longer do I have to live
In a mirage—
You have captivated
Every part of my heart,
Destroyed my brittle thoughts,
Replaced them with
A view of eternity,
And a love for You
That can't be bought.

Oh Lord, make me Your temple

When my thoughts get crowded
I'll throw them away
Into the wind
Into a realm of rubbish
Into the outer space
Anywhere really
So that You may dwell within me
From head to toe—
So that every evil thing outside
Of this tiny being will no longer
Have room within Your home.

I love You now

I loved You
Like I love
New York in the fall
Virginia in the spring
The sand beneath my skin
My toes barely dipped in the sea
With morning fresh air in my hair
The mountain top where I sing
Sipping matcha greener
Than the trees
The pages that reflect me
The roads that raised me
A moonlit night
A sunlit sky
The desire to fly
With closed eyes
That will open mid-fall
As the leaves join me
On the wild ride
Not knowing whether
I'll whisper or shout
For it all depends on
The current state of my heart.
I love You now
More than all these things
Still Your love for me
Has never compared
And will never compare
To earthly things;
It is so much greater than
Everything.

You Are My Everything

If everything I have is stripped away
If I never have all I dreamed of
If I never have anything else
May I always have Christ
If I have Him and all else is gone
Then I still have everything

The audacity of a fool

They will mock you and call you a fool,
But their laughter soon passes,
And the only thing they're left with is gloom.
When they say you're worthless,
Remember, their words aren't long-lasting,
Just like the morning fog.
They run around accusing others
For the things they have done—
And if I'm honest, I feel for them because
I've learned to empathize with their despair,
For I, too, have done great wrong,
And the consequences of
Immorality I've had to bear.
Oh, their vicious minds must be a total torture,
Just imagine living everyday like you're
Headed for doom, what a misfortune—
I understand why they're sometimes
Lonesome and blue.

So woe unto the foolish,
For they're full of futile dreams,
They boast about their gains
And in secret do deplorable things.
Yet they're not only fools because of their
Dreams but for what they wish upon others—
Destruction, violence, and all
That's in between.
My darling, they will try to tempt you
With their "glorious" treasures,
Offer you the desires of your heart,
Bow down and worship you—
Only to trap your soul and destroy your life.
So be wary of the gloating measures
They use to trick those with a weak mind,
For they know they're headed
Towards the ruins, yet they have the audacity
To drag anyone along—
Without remorse or shame,
They smile at the thought of poisoning lives,
And carry all the daggers and knives
That were planted by another fool
On their once fully fleshed heart.
My darling, feel for them,
But don't be fooled by their empty promises,
And don't let their wicked words
Bring you down—
Don't let the world corrupt your heart.

Why yellow is my favorite color

Sometimes, I think my life is a movie,
Or am I stuck inside a frame?
But why is everything moving?
I'm probably just insane.

All I do now?
Spend my money on things I don't need.
You wouldn't believe,
Yesterday, I smiled at the mirror.
It had been a while.
Skin—
Is this all that we get to see?
Then why do we carve some
People into idols?

How are we any different,
Or are we all the same? And if sameness
Brings about unity, then why am I
Constantly trying to leave?
Is it because I hate conformity?
Or am I aware that sameness will
Never bring about true peace?

For they say no man is
An island,
But I consider myself more
Of a sailboat.
So here I am, finally
Reaching the skerry—

Or at least I thought I was.
Like the fool I am, I said,
"I don't need a lifeguard,
I know how to swim."
And you guessed it,
That's when I started to SINK.

You see, not much matters to me anymore.
I had a lot more emotion back then
When girls proudly made fun of the way I dressed
And boys didn't like me because
They said I was strange. How disgusting.
Now the girls ask, "where did you buy that yellow dress?"
And the boys say, "you look better
When your hair isn't covering your face."
They're posing as my friends,
But I know not much has changed,
They still make fun of me when I turn my head.
So I just smile and pretend
Their flattery made my day,
When in reality,
All their words don't mean as much
To me anymore—
At least not as much as they did yesterday.

So, in golden hues, I remain,
For they bring me comfort and remind me
Of true love and sunset glares.
Of sunflowers, krazy kookie dough ice cream,
And childhood dares.
Of who I am and why I don't go
With the flow of the world—
Finally realizing that I was never sinking;
I was just learning how to stand.

Yellow

Is she happy now?
Or is she the same?
The sun seems brighter now,
More than yesterday.

Planting trees where "love" used to exist,
You wouldn't believe the things I did
For those who threw stones at me.
Sadly, they're all dead and I'm still here.

Oh, how I thank the Lord for His mercy,
Which I don't deserve, still He gave me.
So, to answer your question,
Yes, I've left that frame;
I'm no longer the same.

I'm making plans

To love You for eternity
Not just an instance
Not just a breath
Not just a heartbeat
Not just the time I can spare
Not just when I need You
Not just when all is calm
Not just if my dreams come true
Not just if You
Give me all I want.

I'm making plans to live
In Your will,
According to Your word,
For You know what's best,
And I most certainly do not.
Lord, I want to love You forever,
May that always be
My one true desire,
And may my heart never conspire
Against Your holy law.
May all that I am
Live to praise You
And not for the selfish applause—
For nothing on earth will
Satisfy like You,
My faithful God.

Silent Battle

I threw my cares into the wind
And watched everything go out my window.
This is my quiet place—
The pages, the pen,
The words I thought were never meant to be read.
From inaudible cries at night
To blank stares during the day.
My silent battle.
It's not like me to share with the world,
But let's be honest—
Not a single soul might ever read these words,
And I must decide if I'm okay with that.
I think I am…

I now understand,
This lonely process is helping me find the healing
That I need if I want to continue
Pouring out to the world.
But we tend to see it as selfish
When we take time for ourselves,
Or at least that's how I've felt
Throughout this journey.
I just know I couldn't continue giving anymore
If I didn't step back—disappear for a while.

I'm still silently fighting my battles,
Hoping that one day I'll find the courage
To scream to the world that I've overcome
Because my Savior overcame the cross—
Where He bore my sin and shame.

Update
(a few months later)

All the empty pages filled with words
That are not yet alive.
My life falls short of the world's expectations,
Only markings on its walls.
Thankfully, its opinion doesn't matter to me anymore,
It doesn't seem to matter at all.
And fading was my heart of "gold"
Until my story began to unfold,
Oh my Lord, I have now overcome.

Distant friend, I hope you understand,
Jesus became my safehouse, my healing ground,
My Savior, my one true friend.
And He has given me (obviously everything)
This little, precious gift
(The ability to put my thoughts into words)
(Little, because it doesn't compare
To the gift of His mighty word)
Wrapped up in grace and love.
But tell me, is it crazy to think that anyone
Would ever be interested in anything I'd write or say?
It most definitely is, right?
Well, I might not ever publish this.
If so, then this will truly be a silent battle.
Or maybe, just maybe
I'll find the courage to share a little with the world,
For this process has brought about a complete healing,
The kind the world needs but only the Father can give.
So, the best piece of advice I could give you is to
Diligently study and apply His word, be more interested
In what He has to say, not in error-prone words,
And most certainly, do not seek the dirty things of this world.

—

Was I two-faced?

If your life were to become a movie,
Who would you play?
With the thieves, liars, and chiefs on the loose,
Who would you pretend to be?
Or would you choose a different identity?
One I haven't yet seen?

Honestly, it doesn't matter anymore,
You've shown me enough to know
That I'm not here to stay—
There will be a change
Somehow, someway.

O$_2$

You're all I need

You're all I want

You're my oxygen

Far away idol

As if carrying my bones weren't enough, he said,
Imagine draping a whole family on your shoulders,
Having them rely on you but feeling like
You will never have someone to rely on,
And you're left swimming
In the tear-filled lake, lonely and scared,
Surrounded by bodies but not ever feeling their warmth,
Providing but not ever expecting anything in return.
It's burdensome at its best
And wishful thinking at its worst,
For it's easier to continue living
The same way everyday
Than to have a mind that's plagued
By a future you may never get.
They all said it was too unrealistic—
Too far away.

Unreachable, even for the luckiest folks in the world.
Just dream and forget, stuff it under your bed
And pretend it never saw the light of day, they said.
How can they expect me to live with no regrets?
Is it selfless if I didn't choose this life for myself?
The bones are piled high
From all the dead hopes that ran out of time,
So I lit a match and burned
Whatever remained
Because I know it will always be
Far, far away—

For a small-town guy with dreams from east to west,
Now I just trace the forlorn streets in my head
Of the places I thought I would see
On my way to my destiny,
But it all slipped right out of my hands.
Before I could even blink,
My future played a movie.
One of those that leaves you
Sleepless for an endless number of nights,
Senseless for at least a couple of days,
And breathless for a few seconds
That seem to last a lifetime.
And when it's all over—
You're left with a cloud hanging over your heart,
Reminding you of everything you kept behind,
For the ones you love matter more
Than any dream you could ever have.

And as the years passed,
I acknowledged and understood
That I was the one who chose this life all along,
For how could I ever choose a different path—
This one has brought me a great deal of sorrow
That turned into peace and happiness over time,
Everything one could ever desire—
In life.

The desert my father dreamt of

The desert my father dreamt of,
I got to see it with my own eyes.
I had to endure it for some time,
But I knew it was my Heavenly Father's
Way of preparing me for the harsher
Drought that would eventually come—
So when the time came,
In Him, we lacked nothing.

My favorite chair

It is now.
I believe
The time has come
That I
Must sit in my chair and stare into
The nothingness
Where life kisses your forehead
And treachery takes you by the hand.
Leap.
Or take a fiddling step.
Make a change, of some way,
Even if it seems for the worst.
I tell myself,
Anything is better
Than a soul lost
Or hope gone.
The boards creak
Under my fidgeting feet,
Should I make a move?
If I stay,
I know I will lose my mind.
So I stood up,
Grabbed a hatchet, destroyed
What once was my favorite chair.

I once was lost
But now I'm found

In the process of "finding" herself,
She lost herself—
In her eyes an empty stare,
Her soul and body left bare,
Her moonlike smile no longer seems to shine,
Is she running out of time?

She's running in despair—
There seems to be too much damage to repair.
Wondering, who could fix me now?
She says, all my wrong doings I avow,
For I need a miracle to save me,
That is my only plea.

My will to live is slipping away,
But I'll keep hoping for one more day,
For the longing to find peace has remained
Even though my heart continues to be maimed
Time after time—
Oh, what a punishable crime.
So what can I do now?
How can I be found?

I've heard of the One who calms the sea,
Can He calm the storm within me?
Does He know I'm living in tormenting pain?
Can He search my heart and rid me of sin and shame?
Will He guide me to abundant life
Where there will be no more strife—
And build a home in my heart
So that we'll never be worlds apart?
For I've heard that if I live in Him, and He in Me,
I will have eternity.

She was finally found
By a love so profound—
And she says, while trying to "find" myself,
I was found by the One who's always there to help.
Nobody knows me better than He,
Who calmed the storm within me.
And everything I once was, died at sea,
For I have been set free.

Mask

Apathy is the best disguise for the human race,
Said the lovers wearing a mask
To hide the lackluster in their eyes.

Actually, apathy is the worst disguise for the human race,
Said lovers as they took off the mask
To reveal the misery on their faces.
…

Well, I think apathy is the world's disguise
For its sin and shame, what now seems appealing will yield
An unspeakably heavy burden they'll soon have to share.
Even still, acceptance is all they live for and crave—

On earth only, of course.
For in this world, the bad is considered good,
But don't dare call the good by its name
Because having their ears tickled is what most
Of the human race likes instead—

And hiding the truth has become a fashionable trend.
But the lies are being exposed by His glorious light.
Therefore, the truth will prevail—
So is it not for the best to believe
In the God whose majestic power has no end?

Slothful

My life is a balancing act
Where I'm also juggling
One hundred things at once—
Yet being in this lockdown
Makes me feel like I'm stuck
In a lazy town
With so many ideas and
Nowhere to test them out.

So, is it productivity,
Or is it keeping
My mind in overdrive?
Am I being ostentatious
When I tell others that
I'm doing so much
If doing very little
Nowadays seems to
Wear me out?

It's pretty clear, I'm stressed out—
Is it because I only have a dime?
Or am I really running out of time?
Ugh, my mind is overtired,
But my thoughts never seem to stop.

I feel like I'm doing
Nothing at all,
But why are my days
Never long enough?
Is my mind full of trash,
Or are my ideas worth writing down?
So what will it be of me tomorrow
If I don't start now?

I ask myself these questions
Every day, every boring hour,
Every fleeting millisecond—
Because it feels like
I've been walking for miles,
But I'm somehow still stuck
In the same old place.
I just hope that
It's never from a lack of work.

Numbers are for equations

Darling,
Numbers are for equations,
Not your imagination.

They're not your value,
They're not your life.

Humans have manipulated
Numbers to trick you into
Buying things you don't
Need, not even want—

To feed their poison
To anyone they can trap.

So don't let them ensnare you,
And don't count down the days.
Don't worry about yesterday,
Tomorrow, not even today.

For there's an ephemeral
Nature to life on earth,
But in eternity—
There's no such thing as
Counting nights and days.

So why live in constant
Dismay if you believe in
The One whom our price
Has paid?

Precious Moments

My dear friend,
In this very moment,
I wish I could embrace you
With all my love.
Oh, how your beauty shines,
For the sum of the sun, the moon,
And the stars still don't amount
To our Father's radiance.
And although no one is as beautiful as He,
What does it feel like to know
That in His image you were created?
For you were carefully crafted,
Your worth is far above a precious stone.
He's the author of your story,
The perfect word when you feel alone.
And I just hope you understand
That the value is not in men
But in Him alone.
So what does it look like to be
Called His own?
And when you feel broken,
There's no need to worry,
There's no need to be afraid.
He's the Alpha and the Omega,
A healer, a counselor, a father,
A great friend—
The One who justifies, restores, and repairs,
For He's the only One who can save,
Bringing peace and joy to those in despair.
So what does it look like to know and serve
The Savior of the world?

The posture of surrender

You see, your beauty
In this temporal world
Is standardly measured
By earthly women and men,
But I see true beauty
Measured by the Creator;
It has no end.
So stop hiding behind
Mirrors, stop believing
The lies, we were born with eyes,
Yet it seems most are blind,
For very few seek to understand,
And almost none seek wisdom,
But it seems many chase
Money or some kind of fame.
And some want a different body,
Even a different face.
Isn't it enough to know that
The Creator made us in His image,
According to His likeness,
To rule over every beast
In the land, sky, and sea,
Over every creeping thing?
It is, yet few recognize their duties
And most certainly fail to realize
That true beauty lies within—
For you could have a pretty exterior,
But it doesn't compare to the beauty
Found in the posture of surrender;
A contrite heart before the Lord.

A Marvel

I've sat on this park bench
Every morning and afternoon
For the past couple of days,
Hoping my wife won't find out
Anytime soon—
That work set me on fire
So now I have to pretend.
Got my suit on,
Sweating even though I stay in the shade.
Thinking, thinking—
How do I tell her?
But for now, I play a game,
Roll the dice,
And hope life picks me again.

I drift into an autonomous place,
The kind where you marvel at the world—
The endless decisions
Right in front of your eyes,
Before you lose your grip
And it all slips away.
In a matter of seconds,
You think the world is trying
To tear you down.
You say to it—
You owe me everything.
Until reality hits
And you recognize that no one owes you
Anything at all.
Oh my escape, the beautiful scenarios
I make up in my head,
Even they—
Have turned into nightmares.

—

Never been in love

She found herself so alone
That ironically, she would fantasize
About heartbreak all the time,
Wandering—

"What does it feel like to love
Someone so much to the point
Where you wouldn't mind
Losing that love?"

11/08/19

I saw an old man on the street tearing through
The layers of his skin. And time flows through
My veins, an empty cup out in the pouring rain—
The never-ending stories of grace.

Last night, I ran a traffic light, and for a second,
Time seemed to stop, but the reckless thoughts
In my mind never ceased. And there's a
Storm that rages on, a battle won—
Lord, I was lost until You rescued me.

He has a blank stare, chaos emerging.
A kid is now dead, and no one is caring.
Pens are for writing, until they become weapons—

And I was once the girl in a coffee shop
Reading an article on how to be thin.
Tricking the world into thinking that I was
Okay, just because my plate was clean.

It seems we're all empty faces,
Seeking love in all the wrong places—
And that's why I sing.
I was worn out, going crazy, in a frenzy,
Constantly anxious, utterly broken and undone,
Now all my hardships have turned into praise.

My God, You have been so good to me.
I long to tell the stories of others
Who have found hope in You, as I did—

For day by day, I'm learning to trade my
Anxiousness for peace, my reckless thoughts
For thoughts that are pleasing,
My painfilled cries for cheerful singing,
My rebellion for obedience to the Lord.

Twinkling April

April came, and now
She's gone.
She visited, but briefly,
Now I miss her dearly.
She's gone
With the spring
And leaped over summer—
Straight into the autumn breeze.
Every so often,
She twinkles
Like a lonely star at night.
Oh, her sparkle
Can put a smile even on
The grouchiest of guys.
How I miss that light,
How I need those times.
"I wish she visited more frequently,"
I whisper to my shadow
As I wait on the porch steps
For April to come again.

Not yet, Not still

More than words,
More than melodies,
Harder than pretending,
Is to be still
In a world
That shakes
Without relent.

False Hope

The melancholy draping around the shoulders,
How sad that the *light* was actually darkness,
Desolate and destitute—
Walking around with gold on the eyelids
And sparkle on the lips.
Full of false hope with nowhere to call home,
But the city lights were blinding,
And kept taunting—
Calling, at times screaming,
This is your home.

The fake men smile and offer
Nectar sweet to the tongue
But bitter for the soul.
They strut about shining in false glory,
Temporarily unaware that through
His death and resurrection,
The Son of God has melted
Them to the ground—
And they'll forever be stuck and forgotten.

—

The city streets, *golden*—
Eyes gleaming, hearts foolishly trusting.
Only a wise man can tell the difference between pyrite and
The real thing,
But a fool will sell anything and everything
For a plated coin or a pretty penny.

So behold, the poor soul of a skeleton—
Easily mesmerized by paths that will only end up in torture.
For a fleeting moment,
Never having access to a wondrous eternity—
But I now understand, this is exactly how it was meant to be.
False hope is easier to cling to than
The real thing.

Childlike

It felt like a lifetime
Since I last experienced
True happiness.
Swinging in a lonely playground,
Letting go of all my vices.
Finally remembering what it feels like
To have tears from a source other
Than sadness.
Sliding belly down,
Knowing that at the end,
There will be a ground
To catch me,

To watch me
Smile like a giddy child
Who just found out what having butterflies
In the stomach feels like.
It was nice,
For a moment to feel childlike.
Leave this battlefield
That is my mind behind;
The never-ending war
Where I sometimes try to escape
Or fight head-on.
But today, I didn't have the strength to fight,
So I found a way out.
And it was nice,
Even if it was for just a moment.

Can time be squared?

I told you I wanted to live forever,
You told me that was one of your biggest fears—
To live to be so old
That you won't remember all you've lived.
At most, you said you'd like to live till your 40s
And saw yourself digging your grave in your 30s.
I said that was one of my biggest fears—
To die so young
That I would barely have time to breathe.

So can my time be squared?
That way you'll live yours and
I'll take on a second journey—
To carry all our memories, keep them safe,
I promise I will never forget.
I think those were my last words
Before you left.

Oh, how I wish you could know that
I think about you almost every day.
Just yesterday I said,
I wish I would've been a better friend,
But I'm no fool—
I know most wishes don't come true.
But all of yours did, right?
Although now that I think about it,
I knew you well enough to know
That deep down, you didn't wish those things;
We were so young, so naive.

I'm plagued with pain,
Wishing you could get another chance
To rethink your choices—
To live again.
So can our time be squared?
Maybe, just maybe—
In eternity the answer will be yes.
But I know that's my illusive heart speaking
Because to the logical side of my brain
That makes no sense.
For my eyes saw your steps,
My ears knew your ways,
Your hands were always reaching for me,
I was always pulling away—
I knew better than to fall in love
With someone who would never stay.

Tug of War

I'm sick of it

         Right and left

Left and right

         As if it were as simple

As a game of tug o' war

A country where I belong

Yesterday,
I missed the chirping birds outside my window—
That welcome me, call me friend,
And treat me as one of their own,
Temporarily filling that little vacant spot in my soul.
Most days I'm on my own, and although I love to be alone,
I think most people would agree that they hate
The feeling of Loneliness.
How it creeps up at night—
Screaming insanities until it penetrates the mind.
But for me, Loneliness is at its loudest in a crowded room
Full of faces longing to belong.

It all brings me back to yesterday—
Back against the wall, waiting for my order
At my favorite ice cream shop.
Eavesdropping, studying people's faces,
Watching how their eyes sparkle when they talk,
Noticing how quickly a smile comes and goes,
And wondering how long it will take for them to capture
The right image before the ice cream starts to lose its shape.
Everyone was around my age,
With youth and beauty written across their faces,
And I couldn't help but notice that I was the only one
Who was there companionless.

It's in those moments that I feel alone.
But no matter how hard I try
To make friends, to socialize,
I still end up in the same place—
Back against the wall,
The ice cream melting as I stare.

Perhaps it was always meant to be this way;
I've found a great companion in Loneliness,
A comfortability, a safe place.
And I genuinely prefer being selective
Than to be surrounded
By the wrong crowd and praised,
For I've learned that flattery is a fool's favorite game,
But the wise know not to play.

So now I sit and wait, with the knowledge that
My forever home is not too far away.
Therefore, I treasure the ones I love
And spend time with the birds
That taught me how to fly freely
And to never settle in a nest that's less
Than what my Father has to offer.
For I'm seeking a heavenly homeland;
A citizenship to a country splendidly prepared
For those He has chosen to save—
Oh, this divine place where I'll endlessly praise
And enjoy His presence every second of every day.
Of course, I don't know if time is a concept there,
But what I truly know is that I don't know much at all.
Still, I know it's not a wonder that I feel like
A foreigner, a nomad—
Nowhere on earth will I belong.

We are the clowns at the circus

During quarantine, some of us
Complained about being stuck at home
For a couple of weeks,
Maybe a couple of months.
Yet we delight in seeing animals in captivity—
In small cages without the freedom
To roam around. It's heartbreaking to think
That some have never known and
Will never know what grass feels like,
How the sun and moon shine,
Or how the ocean looks at night.
Yes, they were created for us to admire,
Take care of and love,
But never for us to exploit
And keep behind bars.
How I fear what we've become—
So attached to the increasing evil
In our hearts,
Encapsulated by our own
Selfish desires.

Or is this what we've always been?

Quiet Spaces

You're the ever-moving God,
You go everywhere I go,
You are with me in every step I take.
Yet there's a stillness about your love
That keeps drawing me closer,
Pulling me apart from
The things of my past
That brought shame into my heart.
Now, I can confidently say
Your holy love is undoing
All my shameful pride.
So I fully trust and know
That in the quiet spaces,
You're still working;
I can finally rest assured.

You'll never change

I remember the moment
When things began to change—
For You've set me apart, set me to sail.
Despite all my sin and unworthiness—
You've been merciful,
And Your love pours out without fail.

So this is my assurance:
Even when the winds and
Tides grow stronger—
Jesus, You'll never change.

For Your love is like a steady ocean,
And Your holiness never ends.
Forever, You will be
Enthroned in glory—
Worshiped and praised.

So why should my heart worry,
Why should my heart fear
The changing tides and wind?
The Almighty reigns forever—
He is the Alpha and the Omega,
The anchor and the shield.

Will He not sustain me?
Will He not calm the storm
Within me, no matter the trial
Or how big the ache is?
He will—
For He cannot deny who He is.

The real thing
(my one true friend)

Growing up—
Well, it was hard to make friends.
My classmates made fun of
My calves, my chin, my eyebrows,
The way I dressed, the way I walked,
The way I talked—
I couldn't say a word
Without being criticized and made fun of.
But You were with me through it all,
Never was I forsaken or forgotten.

So thank You, Heavenly Father,
For being my one true friend,
For always being there
On my lonely days
And in my crowded May—
Although many have left,
I know You will never depart.
So even when the world decides to
Hate me all the more,
I will always have You,
And that's more than enough.
I rest in Your goodness, Your grace,
And I hope to live there
Every second of everyday.
For what You have taught me,
Given me, and how You love me,
It's all real—
My God, You are real,
There's no denying it.

The real thing
(ashes and dust)

From the freshly cut grass beneath my feet
To the lilac skies above,
The sunflowers reaching towards the sun,
The luminous full moon, the crystal rivers,
The scarlet sunsets that remind me
Of the good that is to come—
Everything, everything
Points to Your existence.
So I close my eyes, take a deep breath,
And while smiling, I extend my arms
Towards the heavens,
Enjoying the time You've given me
On this little place called earth.
All the heartfelt moments,
The silly conversations—
But not the messy nights
When the fight in my mind
Is about to start
And I have front row seats every time.

Oh Father, those nights terrify me—
Please don't ever leave my side.
You know the unsettledness
Every battle brings along,
And how tempestuous
My soul tends to become.
But no matter how difficult the struggle,
May I never deny who You are
And what You've done.
For it's all too real, You are too real,
Yet the world keeps denying it
Time after time.
And my heart will keep on breaking
While simultaneously rejoicing
For the sake of who You are
And what You've done,
Oh, Your Son's sacrifice on the cross—
Till I am nothing but ashes and dust.

SOS

I go to the mountains
To escape—
Scream all the ugly
My tongue creates
With the words
That foolishly prance around
In my head.

I've fooled no one but myself.
I'm going insane.
Lord, Your servant calls for help.

Yellow Brick Road

On the road to recovery,
One must tread carefully;
A single wrong turn,
And you're back at the beginning.
But every road has an end;
May we choose the end wisely.

Sometimes I
Run back to my old habits—
It hurts falling
Into the pit again.
It feels dark and lonely,
Although I know there are others
Who have lived here
Based on the tally marks on the wall,
The shouts of despair
That echo their way to me,
The visuals my mind
Paints with grey ink—
Hoping for the day when everything
Will be multicolored and bright.
A healed body and mind is
The future I see;
I refuse to believe anything else.

I hope you understand that if you're
Struggling with an eating disorder,
An addiction, some sort of mental illness,
Or any other thing—
There is hope, there is a path to recovery,
Believe for it;
We can overcome this.

Songs of Songs

And one day—
We'll look back, smile, and sing
Songs of redemption,
Songs that give glory,
Songs that are healed.
Whether our stories are similar
Or completely different,
This one thing I know—
Empathy should have no end;
We need to share in our sufferings
And encourage each other
To the very end.
So as I throttle the internal struggles,
I will continue writing with hope
And transparency from the comfort
Of my four white walls,
Knowing that what is to come
Is so priceless
Because my Heavenly Father
Has promised it to be—
For you and me,
But only if we join the
March towards eternity.
I know I will,
I will sing,
Will you please join me?
For the harmony only adds beauty
To the melody,
And eternal is the melody
Of the Mighty King.

In the silence

He is deaf to all their threats;
Therefore, he doesn't owe them a reply.
But even in the silence,
The mockers got their last laugh—
Until he crushed them
With the palm of his hand,
Not once saying a single word.
He walked away, head held high,
Leaving all his troubles behind—
The bruises, the words that had cut him
Deeper than a sharpened knife.
But deep down he wondered
If evil for evil would cost him his life.
And in the stillness of the night,
Getting even no longer felt right.

Iceberg

It feels like I'm coming apart at the seams;
I'm giving everything,
But is there even anything left to give?
I know there's so much more
Left unexplored, left unseen,
Can You please show me what it is?

I've been sinking in cold water;
Your sun is melting me—
Is this how it's meant to be?
I'm sorry for questioning everything,
But I need clarity.

It feels like everybody just sees
The ugly parts of me
That are trampled and dirty.
But the lovely lies below—
Pure, white as snow.

So why do I feel the need
For others to see what only You can see;
Is it not enough,
For me to live just for You
And not the earthly things?
It is, it should always be.
And the water suddenly
Became clear—

I need to uncover every part of me,
Especially the unexplored, the unseen.
But first, I need to let go
Of many things so that I
May step into territory unknown
And frightening, very enlightening,
But equally purifying.

I'm going,
Drifted by Your Spirit—
Your love casting out my fears.
I'm turtle-paced,
But I'm getting there,
Even if I must melt a little along the way.

Oh, the formidable journey—
The beginning to my end,
Although there were moments
When I danced on the waves,
But now time remains still—

Frozen,
Till I understand.
There's so much left to give
There's so much left to see
There's so much left to do
There's so much left to grief.

I'm learning to stand firm
With the sun smiling down at me,
As I thaw in the sorrow,
Holding on to the hope
Of a tomorrow…

And surely,
Joy came at dawn
When the sea creatures
Began to spawn—
New life bloomed in every corner,
And I became a tranquil river
That trickles into the vast ocean.

Fresh air

I'm much happier these days.
I love living,
I love breathing the fresh air—
The morning walks,
The nightly talks,
My life with You has changed;
I'm no longer exasperated
When things don't go my way.

So I hop on the boat and don't look back,
Leaving the waves behind,
The Holy Spirit guiding me to righteousness,
Allowing me to understand things that are
Unfathomable to the senseless mind.
I arrive, and quickly get to know the land.
Then, I become one with the leaves,
Drifted by Your wind,
The Good News falling on dry bones,
Men falling to their knees,
Leaving it all behind to follow the King.
Oh Lord, what a joy it is to grow closer to You;
To know You like never before,
To profess faith publicly and behind closed doors.
To live by faith and not by sight,
Believing that Your will for us is better
Than anything our flesh could ever want.
And trusting that with Your word, the parched land
Will yield a great harvest in the spring,
For You hold all the power to give life
To the dead and lowly.

Prodigal

A father's desire is to gain
His children's love and trust
So that they may stop wasting time
Thinking about ways to escape,
So that they may stop roaming
Aimlessly like a bird that
Wanders from its nest.
Oh, that they may find freedom
And redemption in Christ Himself.

So reassuring them, he said—
I understand, you're probably
Tired of running in the wild,
But you can finally rest
And not waste
Everything you've been given
On people who want to stealthily
Steal your health.
Oh my child, there's no longer a need
To be afraid, to keep running,
To waste your youth on meaninglessness,
To feel unbeautiful
And alone in this world,
For the Son came to pay the price;
Thus, there's no lack of plentifulness in Christ.

Then he shouted, as his eyes filled
With tears so heavy
They could pierce the earth—

I love him
Like I almost lost him;
He had his wings clipped off
So I taught him how to swim,
How to love,
How to seek redemption
So that he may finally be free,
And at last, he has been set free.

I love her
Like I almost lost her;
I found her broken,
She was quite the disaster,
So I prayed incessantly,
And thankfully,
He gave her a new mind,
A new heart,
And a spirit that can't be crushed.

For a father's desire is to watch
His children live in the posture of surrender
Before the Lord, knowing that He will
Take care of the rest, fully trusting
That when they leave the nest,
They'll never be attracted to the feculent
Things of this world.

In my head

I felt gone, empty
Since that day in November.
But the word reminded me
To take a step in faith,
For there's no greater reward
Than eternity with Him.
So I jumped, I leaped.
I took the biggest step
Of my life
And came to an understanding
Of what being Spirit-led
Looks like.

You see, in my head
Was a scary place to live;
You wouldn't want to see
The things that were on repeat.
But thanks and praise be to God,
For He set me free from
The thoughts that once captivated me.

Eternal Song

In the forever I belong,
Like a father and daughter
Dancing at her wedding
To the beat of an eternal song.
Doe-eyed and full of life,
Soaring on the wings of eagles,
Leaving old earth behind.

Looking towards the promised paradise,
Wondering, if I close my eyes,
Will I almost see it—
But its beauty is unimaginable,
Too grand for any human brain
To dance around.
Until then, I will march
To the beat of the eternal song.

School's Trigger

Never saw myself pulling the trigger,
Never thought I would be on
Either side of the gun—
What a wasteland we live on
If it's just to collect dust.
But summer comes early,
And I'm overcome with the
Fear of returning,
Once again—
To the brook that
drowned me,
Later the lighthouse
I tried to climb—
Year after boring year,
Meticulously planning
For the end to draw near.

Evening Shadows

The wicked tread a treacherous road,
Their slimy hands crave all that is gold.
They do not fear what is to come;
Their hearts are rotten, and their minds have succumbed
To the deadly gaze of their haughty eyes,
For evil is their most glorious prize.
Therefore, their days will never grow long
Like the evening shadows,
Yet they sin like they have a tomorrow—
Strutting around in complete darkness,
Avoiding the gallows,
And seeking to prey on the righteousness
Of those who eagerly want to live and die for Christ
And follow His sound advice—
But they will never get it right,
For their minds are destined to ignorance and spite.

So woe unto them—
The ones who do not understand,
For no amount of wickedness can satisfy
Their thirsty soul and disdainful eyes.
Oh, the heaviness they carry in their hearts
Has led them to become bitter and tart.
Thus, their story will end in the shadows;
For them, there'll never be a tomorrow.
Therefore, the only time they have is now—
This is their chance to lay their earthly treasures down.

The Bear and its cave

Dreading the darkness, I said to myself,
How long must I keep living alone?
Too many years have passed,
So my fears turned into stone,
From which I crafted a beautiful home.
But what good is a beautiful home
If I don't have friends who visit me?
If my slumber only produces fantastical
Dreams that never become reality?
If I spin the frames to extract
The honey that ends up sticking
To my fur, then realize there's no one
Here to enjoy the process with?
And with all my fur, oh, the amount
Of warmth and love I could give.
But I fear accidentally letting
The hunter near, him skinning me
For selfish pleasure, or me devouring
Him because meat is nourishment
Into my bloodstream. Yet the word says,
One mustn't live by bread alone,
So if this loneliness will bring me closer
To Thee, then let it be just You and me.
And grant me enough faith to see
Beyond this cave, beyond the grave,
Beyond my animal instincts.

Honey

I was its sweet delight
Called me honey and
Licked me dry
Stole my joy
And left me
Grey and sad
Still asked me to stay
Asked me for a chance
Begged me for a dance
That I refuse to give again
…

Freedom from perpetual sin was one of
The many great things that happened to me
On the day the Lord opened my eyes
So that I wouldn't continue living in darkness.
Now I'm able to recognize that His grace is plenty,
That His love is more than enough,
That His words are truly sweeter than honey,
And that He is the Light of the world—
So like a city on a hilltop,
May I reflect His light,
And in every corner, with no reservations,
Praise His holy name day and night,
For His power is made perfect
In my weakness—
I no longer have to rely
On my own fragile strength.
Oh, blessed is He forever and ever, amen.

Spaced-out teeth

Her chubby cheeks and spaced-out teeth
Remind me of innocence and what it means
To live carefree. With rainbow shoes,
Floral pants under a purple dress,
Messy hair, oh how fun it is for a child
To get to dress itself. I wish it were as easy
For me to not worry or care about what
Others will think, instead of thinking,
"Will this highlight my belly?
Will my crooked teeth be too noticeable
If I smile big? Does red go with blue?
Does pink go with green?"
Why does it even matter?
Why don't I do and wear what pleases me;
Even better, why don't we do what pleases
The Father and desire His will,
And just wear the butterfly socks,
The mismatched outfits, or the carefully
Matched outfits, and smile as big as a bright
Half-moon on a clear, summer evening.

Leave

The trees stand in complete silence as I fall,
A fall that never seems to end.
The hustling wind I blame;
My grip was stronger than its rage.

This, I'm sure of; I've held firmly
Through endless rain,
Although I wouldn't know of fire
Since I've only crossed paths
With its mistress—
The spark that never turned into a flame.
And I'm glad because
It would've been my disgrace.
She doesn't know how to love,
So she destroys everything in her way.

Finally, I kiss the earth—
Her taste of dirt and old age,
Just like I remember it.
I breathe in and exhale,
And just like that, the seasons change.

Green fades into a memory
When autumn announces its return.
Now, I can blend in
With the hues that fall into the trend.
And I wonder when and how my life will end
And if I lived a life of righteousness—

I hear laughter in the distance,
It sounds so much louder
Than how I remember it
From up there.
Suddenly, something fills me with worry,
Panic runs through my stem—
Wishing I could somehow grow legs
To run away.

The day seems to turn into night—
And I wonder, why so fast?
As everything around me
Grows completely dark,
I hear—crunch, crunch, crunch.
My life seems to have ended
With the trampling of little innocent feet
That weren't even seeking revenge;
Now, there are too many pieces
To try to put my life
Back together again.

So the best advice I could give is—
Leave before it's too late.
After all, I hope I lived a life
Worthy of being born again
In a land where I won't be crushed,
And I will finally be safe.

But seriously, leave right now
Everything that's holding you back
From following The Maker—
I promise it's the best decision
You will ever make!

Don't let your downfall become your grave.
It's not a pretty place
To crawl in the dirt amongst the worms—
They will eat your flesh; trust me,
I've learned this from past mistakes.
...

I opened my eyes
And realized that it was all just a dream—
Or a nightmare, I should say.
I sighed with relief—
Deliberately making sure that
My grip was stronger than ever
And my faith—forever unshakeable.

Grey November

Lost in the Grey November
My feathers are gone from
Braving the weather
Oh where do I run to?
Where do I run to?

Change or death
Who tips the scale?
My mind succumbs
When my heart
Becomes stale
Oh who do I run to?
Who do I run to?

If I could fly to the highest peak of a mountain
If I could swim to the depths of the ocean
If I could hide in the darkest cave
If I could get lost in the wilderness
If I could migrate with the birds
If I could change my identity
And move somewhere else

Would I find peace?
Would my heart mend?
Would You find me there?

You found me

How foolish of me
To think I could hide from Your love.
How foolish of me
To belittle what You have done
Even though I know Your grace
Is more than enough.

How many tears have You cried?
How many times have I saddened Your heart?
It breaks me, I fall apart—
I don't want to hurt the One I love.

But I keep running away,
I keep playing games,
It's hide and seek all day
Every day till I grow tired
And partly lose my hair,
Then I'm left collecting the strands that serve
As a reminder of my unworthiness—
Of the "much" I've lost in this fictitious world.
And as I look around, I can see why this house
Overflows and aches with abandonment.

Oh, Father, I need a companion—
A friend that will stay.
I need a true home—
One where I won't feel like a pest.
So can You be my place of rest?
Are You my sacred nest?
Indeed, You are.

Please forgive me, for it took me a while
To realize that all I need is found in You.
I was too busy chasing folly,
Only for it to lead me away from the truth.
So how foolish does one have to be
To deny Your love?
A love freely given, untainted,
Never unmoored.
Well I know, for how foolish of me
To ever think I could run or hide from such
Wholesome love.
But look at me now—
Rolling around in green meadows,
Drinking from peaceful streams,
Fully known, fully free,
Abundantly loved and healed.

Oh, Father, You found me
Amongst the rubbish, nevertheless,
You gave me lovely sisters and brothers
So that I would never feel alone.
And I'll never have to hide or run,
For I'm a new creation
Revealed by Your grace—
And yes, I'm still unworthy,
But a fool, I no longer am.

Once a stranger

My spring overflowed with
Lifeless water,
Her taste bitter for my soul,
Still, I didn't want to spill any for love.
But You took me in despite
My bitterness and brokenness.
You purified the water
In the streams of my mind,
Gave life to the broken parts
Of my once-tainted heart,
Showed me what true love looks like,
And gave me bones that
Will outlast the test of time.
And as the years came to pass,
I started knowing You, loving You,
Revering You more and more with every breath.
Thus, I no longer live like a stranger in the mire,
Yet You've always known me;
I've always been Your daughter.

When the world goes silent

She says I remind her of autumn in Venice
Or summer in Tulum.
Quiet in her mannerisms,
Boisterous in the way she loves.
It breaks me, her voice,
I don't recognize it anymore.
My surroundings have become numb,
And the ringing in my ear is now unbearable,
Like a pestering menace,
Like a fly that keeps landing on your food.
I stay quiet because if I speak,
My voice will drown out the moon,
And in her eyes, the last glimmer of hope
Diminishes to almost nothing.
She feels forgotten, unloved,
Her emotions frozen like creepy gargoyles
On top of an old gothic building.
And the dark of the sky becomes frightening,
Everything she once loved becomes frightening.
I wish I could tell her I feel the same way.
The world grows distant day by day,
Silence follows me in every corner I stand,
And I don't know what to do.

The war in my mind

I am human,
So are *you*—
Doing wrong is so easy,
But is there truly pleasure
In burning the soul?
Now, doing right
Tastes so sweet in my mind,
Yet why don't I choose it
All the time?

Instead—
There's a battle in my head,
One I fight every day.
Three seconds of sin feels *fine*.
Oh, really, just to crawl back
Into the shell I once had?

So why don't I choose to do what
Brings joy to Your heart?
Is it because I don't
Love You enough?

It brings me great sorrow
To think that You cry when I fall,
After all You've done for me,
Even when I say
I'm seeking eternity—

I know of Your merciful love,
I know of my crushing nature,
So why do I continue scavenging
Amongst the things that rot?

I've drank from Your rivers,
I've drank from Your cup,
They're thirst quenching,
They're sufficiently enough.
But there's a war in my mind,
One that has already been won
With the blood of Your Son—

Oh my Lord, You've set me free;
I'm no longer held captive
By the law and my sin.
So teach me how to live for You,
How to love You more,
How to surrender the war
So that I may live with joy and peace—
Fully knowing there's nothing
That could come between
You and tiny me.

Romans 6-8

More than an element

With just the thought of spending
One day apart, I'm exasperated—
Gasping for air, heart beating out
Of my chest, losing my cool—
Oh, is this what if feels like
To burn alive, to lose my mind?

But to think You're
Comparable to oxygen—
Ha! How little is my faith?
Yet how powerful is my God?

For only You give life
And decide when and how
It will come to an end.
Thankfully, I don't need
To worry—my life is secure
In Your mighty hands.

For my Creator is
More than an element,
More than mere words
Can describe—
The only *Holy, Holy, Holy,*
Powerful God.

May You always be
All I need,
All I want.

Mary had a Little Lamb

Jesus, to walk in Your light,
What a delight—
My sweet, sweet,
Precious Jesus,
The righteous Lamb—
How could I ever
Sing enough of Your love?

The tiny white house on the hill

Memories forever cherished—
Running around in the endless space,
Rolling down the hills
And landing on my face.
My basket full of mangoes
That had fallen from the trees,
And when there were none on the ground,
I would climb without the fear of falling,
For childhood fears were no such thing.
On my birthday, I would get a plastic doll
And share it with the other girls in the town
Since their parents didn't make enough
From milking the cows—
The truth is, we also had very little,
But to me, it was always more than enough.

You see, my happiest memories
Were of such a time
When materialistic things didn't matter
As much as they seem to matter now.

So in the empty corridor of
My grandma's clay house,
The children would gather
To play with the rocks we would find—
In the river just down the hill,
Where most of our time would unwind,
We learned how to swim
By trying not to drown.
It was in that very place
Where we imagined ourselves
As mermaids elegantly swimming in a pack,
Laughing when the currents
Would drift us apart, and finding treasures
That no amount of money could ever buy.
There was no animosity or jealousy
In our hearts—
Just children living a pure life,
Enjoying each other's company
And sharing the little that we had.

Those are some of my core memories
From the tiny white house on the hill,
But the adventure is not over,
For there are still so many childhood dreams
I'm chasing and trying to fulfill.

P.S. And to those I left behind—
Growing up was the worst
Current of them all.
But I hope we can gather someday
To retell our memories,
Laugh at our misfortunes,
And share the baggage
We now haul.

I've been greedy, have you?

Have you ever felt like you have
Everything you want and need?
But you're aware that you don't deserve
To have it all, so a tiny part of you wants
To return it, give at least some of it away.
Yet you come up with excuses as to why
You need more and more,
And now you're plagued with guilt
Because the mind is a master of deception;
It cannot be fully content and truly fulfilled.
So you compromise and decide that
It's okay to be greedy, just this one time.
Still, you never ever feel pleased—
There's always an emptiness inside;
A great need that can't be met by
The perishable things of this life.
Well, that's how I used to feel
Until the moment I kneeled and prayed
For forgiveness and mercy,
With a heart postured in surrender,
Finally recognizing that I don't deserve
And could never earn His mercy, love, and grace.
So now that these things have been given to me freely,
I joyously live and abide by His laws—
Because, without Him, life is no life at all.
Therefore, I've come to know that God is the only One
Who will forever be more than enough;
The only One who can perpetually satisfy the soul.
So when the world offers you *everything,*
Please know that it wants to steal from you
And leave you feeling empty and cold.

The Vertex of Seventeen

At seventeen, I thought I had my life figured out.
I would go to university and leave this provincial town.
Drift to places unseen, bright lights
That would make me feel seen,
But deep down I knew that what I truly needed
Was perpendicular to my wants.

Lately, I've been dancing on a bridge.
I'm in the in between; the place in my mind
Where everything seems to be crumbling.
What do I tell the girl who would eat lunch
Alone in a deserted hall?
Although she felt like a nobody—
Her dreams weren't small, yeah, nothing unheard of;
She somehow believed she could do it all.

So once again, the unsteadiness of this bridge
Makes me think about leaving town.
It's all I spend my time on—
The prancing questions of what if, why not, why me,
Why would anybody love a nobody?

But this time, everything feels different.
There's a deep despondency within me
That craves the dark—
Some kind of hiddenness, anonymity, an invisibility cloak,
You name it; I would give everything to not be seen
And in my new town—to never be found.

2nd Vineyard

The vines of entanglement, no one can escape.
They wrap around bodies like the mind
Grapples with Death....

His limbs can't handle the tears,
Her body can't swallow any more pain.
Their minds wrestle with Death every day,
And they echo, keep fighting just a little longer.

I tried to help, but he refused it.
I tried to love, but she pushed me away.
They said it would make them look weak,
They said they would rather die in agony
Than live a new life because, in their minds,
Change is the scariest thing one can face.

So now I just sit and watch
The birds as they migrate south,
Avoiding my frontal view
Because it's unbearable to the naked eye.
And in my melancholic discomfort,
I try to enjoy the fruits of my labor,
But I'll tell you the truth—
There is no joy in the now, for it hurts
With a tantalizing, paralyzing kind of pain
To watch others lose themselves and eventually *die.*

To See Your Face

Four
Years on this earth,
Yet she asks questions
Most adults wouldn't even dare.
She stares at the sky
And proclaims its beauty,
Then with a giant smile on her face,
She says, "I wonder what Jesus' face looks like,
I bet it's beautiful."
And so, she spins till she falls on the grass,
Never failing to point out
Its greenness.

To her, the whole world is beautiful,
Lovely, and sweet,
Yet she cries deeply when
She sees others hurting;
Her heart breaks—
The way our Heavenly Father's heart does
When His children are facing calamity
Or when they're in distress.

She asks questions of the future,
Like, "what does heaven look like?
And what can I do to get there?"
She can barely grasp the concept of death
But says it's too early for her to leave,
And then she proceeds to ask me
If I'm ready to face death and go to heaven,
To which I reply,
"Yes, but only God knows when my time
In this world will end, for He has
Determined the course of my life.
But while I'm still here,
I will wholeheartedly trust Him
And patiently wait."

But to see Your face,
So much light all at once,
Our human eyes can't withstand,
Oh, how I long for that day.
I think about it a lot more now
That my Grace points it out
Pretty much every day,
Reminding me of Your beauty
And what it means to always have
That childlike sense of wonder and faith.

The Garden

The seed broke through,
The garden blooms again.

I saw a spark,
And it turned into a flame.

Dressed in fine linen,
With nothing but a smile on my face.

And I said, He is my first love—
The One I love above all else.

For all will go from dust to dust,
But my Holy Father forever remains.

When I awoke from my slumber,
I planted a garden where life blooms
In every possible color.

I kept it in the dark for some time,
Ironically, that was the perfect way
For it to get enough light.

And so, this strange form of nourishment
Became a mystery to me,
Slowly unraveling before my very eyes—

As I gained more and more understanding
In the silence; in the confinement
Of my once-barren mind.

The secret place between You and me,
I know now that it does exist.

I sang until the night turned to dawn,
Spoke in words not loved by most mankind.

Oh, the prettiest of places I ever did see,
I didn't know it was so close to me—

It's my very own to keep,
My virtual reality—

This Garden,
              Just for You & me.

Mostly Ghostly

There's a mysterious comfort
In feeling like you live
Among the things unseen;
Therefore, I've learned to love
(Perhaps a little too much)
Feeling like a ghost
In a world that loves
To praise the loud and seen.

Nothing under the sun

Everything under the sun
Must come to an end,
This I've learned—
From losing a love
To laying down a friend.
If we all eventually have
The same fate,
Then what's the point of living,
I ask myself—
Chasing the wind, things unseen,
Like birds flying too close to the sun
Or men walking on the moon before Neil,
Houses turning to grey
When ashes are all that remain,
Where a family once stood,
Now they've all gone
Their separate ways.

Nothing under the sun
Lives forever,
So why should I fear death?
If to die is gain,
Why should tomorrow
Bring me sorrow?
I have enough worries for today.
Under the sun, foolishness
Is mostly what I see and hear—
The chasing of material things
Seems meaningless,
So what if I finally catch the wind?
But just like the end of day,
When the light fades,
So will my heart stop beating.
Oh, I mustn't take fright,
For nothing under the heavens
Is here to stay—
But eternity is just a death away.

Where does your soul belong?

Did you really think
You could keep us
Locked in a cage?
That we would never escape?
Oh, how foolish of you;
There's an infallible way
To bend the metal bars
And fly away from the madness
That was never more than
A dirty house.

For the One who is
The way, the truth, and the life
Paid it all, now we can soar in the sky,
Thanking Him for all He has done,
With the knowledge that our true home
Is nearing, the great reward
Reminding us to keep strong,
Never being by chance
That we all find where our souls
Truly belong.

Surefooted

You have made me surefooted
Like a strong dear,
In Your love I'm rooted
As I let Your wind steer—
Therefore, I'll never be led astray,
For Your guidance keeps me safe,
And under Your wings I'll forever stay,
With You, braving the toughest waves,
Giving You all the glory and praise,
Pouring out my worries and pain,
Melting in Your embrace
And never looking back at the train
Of darkness left behind—
For in Your love I'm rooted,
You've given me a new mind,
And I undoubtedly know I'm surefooted,
For I stand firmly on the solid ground,
Promising to never depart
This home of mine I've found—
Right next to Your steady heart.

Mirrors and Lies

There are those who worship mirrors,
There are those who love the lies.
They whisper obscenities to deprave
The mind and weaken the spine.
Their reflections are enough to captivate their hearts.
And I see them pass by—chained, occupied;
Creating paper statues as they fiddle with their gold,
Wondering if it'll go up in value as they get old.

So what happens when their outward beauty fades
And their backbones are no longer straight?
Will they go mad, will they finally be free,
Will they be glad?
But corruption never stops lurking—
Waiting to ambush those with a tainted heart in hopes
Of leading them to insanity; oh, what a sick life.

Tell me, is there a better medicine than a purified mind—
Self-denying, full of compassion and lots of laughs?
Yet who is brave enough to tear down
The gods and goddesses
We've created with our minds, leave the wicked path,
Trade gold for brass, go against the crowd?

The truth is—nobody is brave enough
On their own strength and will.
Therefore, I urge you to cast the crooked crown,
For nothing on earth is of any value—
Even the kings and queens know
That one day, their reign will end.
But an eternal kingdom is on its way.

So what does it mean to love yourself
But not hold on to any pride,
To love others, even the ones who do you wrong?
What does it look like and feel like to love God, above it all,
Even if it means getting rid of everything that's considered
Priceless and invaluable to mankind?

Come on, trade your mirrors for crystal rivers,
Dare to swim upstream, dream to see the unseen,
Throw away your paper gods,
Your greed, your plastic thoughts—
Wipe the fake smiles, stop hiding behind the lies,
And get rid of the immorality born out of a fragile heart.

Tell me, have you ever experienced
The fullness of joy that comes from
The incomparable craftsmanship of the One above?
Look outside, at the green pastures, the autumnal sidewalk
Full of leaves of all different colors.
The periwinkle sky, the wildflowers,
The children playing on the playground.
The furry creatures, the oranges barely holding on,
The beauty in the genuine smile of a stranger.
The crickets at night, the moon when it's visible at 4pm,
The sun when it's covered by the clouds.
Your heart beating faster when you look at someone you love,
Or hearing the cry of your baby for the very first time
After years of struggling with infertility.
Receiving the news that your father is now cancer-free,
And feeling overjoyed because seeing him smile so effortlessly
Means the world to the entire family.
Dreams becoming a reality after working
Hard for what seemed like a lifetime.
Being gifted faith and wisdom when you know
You don't deserve even the dirtiest of dimes.

And trust me, I know there will be heartbreak,
There will be pain, disappointments, deaths,
Lonely nights and days.
But when we come to the light, there is a newfound peace
That surpasses all human understanding.
...

Oh, the endless amount of good that tells us He exists;
Why do we choose to focus mostly on the negative?

The Creator of everything

Thankfully, there are those who worship the Creator
Because they have tasted the water
That forever quenches the thirst and completely satisfies.
So in spirit and in truth, they get rid of what the world
Calls valuable and spit out the lies.

Albeit few and rare, these are the ones who defied the odds
When people pointed at them and laughed at their God.
They dutifully share in His suffering, knowing that no matter
How difficult life is on earth, His promise of eternity
Will always stand and it cannot be compared to anything else
(It is far too beautiful for our little human minds
To picture and fully comprehend.)

But where there's an even, there's an odd;
These are the people who are bitter and aching
Because what the Father gives is the peace they need
Instead of the wars being fought—
They don't live with the kind of love that risks it all
(Although there's no risk in loving and living for Christ,
Only a life of beautiful sacrifice.)
It's the freedom they claim, yet they do not have,
For they are slaves to sin and every evil thing—
But perhaps they'll never have freedom,
And what they'll only know of is tormenting chaos.
(Look, I'm aware of how harsh that sounds,
But the truth will always withstand the lies.
Ultimately, the reason I live is not to be praised or liked,
So please bear with me, I'm just trying to speak my mind.)

I know I've previously urged you
To appreciate the beauty found in creation,
But my heart's sole desire is for you to worship
The only One who is worthy without a doubt.
So come on, I dare you to look outside,
There are branches swaying in the wind,
There's rain falling from the sky.
But also look within, search every corner of your mind,
Spend time vetting every part of your heart—
There's more to life than a mirror, than lies and likes.

Why worship the mortal or the things that break and rust?
Everything man-made can and will crumble to dust.
Just look at His creation; it testifies to
His goodness, magnificence, and power,
So why not worship the Creator of everything?

He, who gave us the wonderful counselor named Jesus,
Who separated the light from the darkness,
Who made every single creature—
Including you and me.
All glory be, to the Creator of everything.

Hangmen

They pay death for death,
If they didn't have a heart,
I would understand, but they cheer louder
When they see a man being hanged,
As if nothing ever mattered before
Because nothing will ever matter again.
And they think vengeance will satisfy them,
So forgiveness leaves the human brain,
For all that they can taste
Is the sweetness of the present,
Not the sour that will remain.
And since they forgot the precedent,
The vicious cycle repeats itself
Again, and again, and again—
Until blood becomes the only thing
These wicked men can stomach;
The only thing that temporarily
Quenches their insatiable thirst.
Therefore, I renounce what the world loves
And mourn the in-crowd,
For they're rotting in their luxurious graves,
Hosting parties and cheering
When the next friend in line is unmistakably dead,
Poisoning their minds and bodies
With sin and selfishness.
So I desperately want to make it clear—
I want no part in this mess.

160

I miss the rain

I've been missing the rain,
And everything I once was
No longer remains. Not even a stain.

Although You already know this,
I think I should tell You that I left
My job in a terrible way,
And the berating never stops;
Many think I'm lazy
Or just insane.

But if I had an option,
I'd rather them think of me as crazy
Because people tend to think
That they know you pretty well,
That your life is rose pink,
And that your water is never stale.
So let them for once say that I am
Unstable and unwell, maybe then
They'll be able to empathize and care.

But when they see you struggling,
They laugh and look the other way,
And still love to claim that they've
Always known you pretty well.

So as I hop on the unemployment train,
I hear the chatter of the so-called friends;
Their opinions of who I am leave me drained.
I don't expect everyone to understand
That what drives me is not always
The tangible things of this world;
Sometimes it's every grain of sand
I can hold with one hand,
But other times—
It's the reminders in the wind,
The melodies that dig past my skin,
And the tender whisper of the moon's voice
That drowns out the darkest of noise,
For it hurts to be called lazy,
But I'm choosing to look past the hazy
Parts of life that will drive one mad,
I don't want to end up bitter and sad.

Therefore, I won't take the easiest path
Or what others think is best or right.
I will choose what I need and not what I want,
For the driver of this train has only
Good things planned; if not on earth,
Then it's for sure in the afterlife.
Thus, I know deep in my bones—
Lazy is what I'm not.

Oh Father, forgive me for thinking such things
When I know You've given me wings
To work in Your kingdom relentlessly
And fly into the atmosphere
Without hesitancy—
Where the rain I've been dearly missing
Feels oddly warm to the touch
And oh, so near.

Oh dreary fear

You painted a beautiful sunset inside a frame,
But I told you I no longer live in things that resemble boxes
Or things that remind me of what it was like to be ensnared,
So stop trying to keep me *safe*.

I'm torn between
Two desires

To live or to die.
Dying would ease my pain
And I would finally leave
Every one of my worries behind,
Get to be with You day and night,
In Your presence forever reside.
But to live a long, healthy life
Is an honor I can take on,
For it means I'll get to work
A little longer in Your kingdom,
Bringing the Good News
To the lost souls on this crooked
Earth who desperately
Need to hear it right now—
In hopes that they will receive
Understanding, and at last be found.

So, after pondering for some time,
It's clear that both desires
Have a glorious hope—
A promise of eternity
Since there's no condemnation
For those found in Jesus Christ.
Thus, I do not know which is best;
Both bring great peace and joy
To my heart—
And remind me not to worry
Or rush this precious time of mine
Because the outcome is set in stone;
I know I'll forever be surrounded
By Your grace and love.
So whether I live a long life
Or You were to take me right now,
May my desire always be
To live in Your will,
Praising You no matter what comes.

Flattering Lips

Cut off the flattering lips,
Rip out the deceitful heart,
Allow yourself to be purified
Like gold in a fiery furnace and
Catch yourself feeling terrified
When you discover that you
Didn't fully burn in the fire;
Only your mouth turned into ash,
But that was part of the plan.
And with the passing of time,
Your tongue will become
Reflective and wise—
So that your words may be
As sweet as a honeycomb,
So that your lips come back
Full of melodious sounds,
With a heart that expands
Towards the Savior;
The One who will forever
Keep your mind safe
From every fawning lie.

All I've Feared
(at the end of my road)

Sometimes, I'm frightened by the thought
That my songs may never be heard
And my words may never be read.
Sometimes, I fear that I'll never be good enough,
I'll never find love, I'll never have true friends.
At times, I feared that I'd never be happy again,
But happiness always came.

All I've feared, many things, too much to list—
Yet I'll never fear losing Your love,
Your abounding peace,
All the beautiful things You give,
For what You give, You have given
Freely and wholly.
And all that You have undone within me
Adds to my never-ending list of reasons to rejoice,
For I know that when You redeem,
You do it completely, so I wholeheartedly trust
That You'll never forsake me,
That You'll love me eternally,
And that Your guidance will keep me safe.

Oh, my perfect Lord, leaving this path
Will never cross my mind again,
For I now undoubtedly know
That at the end of my road,
I'll be with You, my precious Jesus,
My righteous Lamb—
All that I'm becoming is because of
Who You are and what You've done.

To plant a seed

For every need
Plant a seed
In the mire
Ignite a fire
In the rain
Pour out your pain
And learn to love
What comes from above

Teach others how to plant a garden
And how to give genuine pardon
Lead them to the path of righteousness
So that they may forgo their mindlessness

Plan to grow and never wilt
Learn to let go of all your guilt
Everywhere you go, always bloom
And watch your doubt fade like brume

For my child, I want your roots to grow deep
So with every need, don't forget to plant a seed

On the mountain top

I stand here in awe
Of Your creation,
The way You hand painted the sky,
How You made the sunflowers yellow,
And how yellow always reminds me
Of how Your love makes me feel.

Every mountain has a different
High and low,
The trees whisper to me
A new song,
And I know I should keep my eyes open
To try to take it all in,
But I close them because a part of me
Can't believe You made all this
For humanity.
I am unworthy—
I see the great disparity
Between You and me.

Yet You have not forsaken me,
With tenderness You look at me
Even though I'm not anything special;
There's nothing worth looking at within me,
For I am a lowly thing
And You are almighty.
But in the gentleness of a moment,
You remind me
That I was made in Your image,
And all that's intrinsically within me
Will continue to die
So that I may be holy like You, my God.
Therefore, I open my eyes and decide
It's okay to take it all in;
That's the reason You handcrafted
The land, the sky, the sea—
For us to take care of and enjoy
Every detail, eyes wide open.

Your creation, I'm in awe—
Every creature, river, stone, grove,
Weird-shaped leaf;
It baffles me how,
In just one second, You make me
Feel loved, treasured, and seen.
But that is who You are—
The epitome of an artist,
A loving father,
A caring friend,
Everything I could ever need;
My inspiration for every
Word, painting, and melody.

The Helper

In this house, we groan, with burdens
Made light, we persevere beyond our words
As hope is a reality made alive through
The Spirit, who helps us in everyday ways,
In which path to take—
Always the right one, of course.

...

My head slips through the hole in my sweater,
And I come out seeing on the other end,
Smiling because joy lives within,
And all the fruits of the Spirit are ready for harvest
As they soon will stroll through the markets,
Ready to instill sweetness into the hearts
Of those who have never tasted anything
Better in their lives.

So I get in the car and go for a drive,
On my way, I notice the gentle patience
That sits with the old man who rocks back
And forth in his green chair, garage door open,
Whether there be sunshine or rain,
Reading the word. I smile at him, but he's too
Preciously busy to look up. So I giggle and cry
A gentle cry, for the Spirit lives within those
Who honor Him, come day and night.

It's all my Father's doing; what a splendorous plan,
For the homeless a home, for the orphan a family,
For the lonely a mighty friend.
Oh the Helper, He shows me the way,
For He abides in me, and I in Him,
Bringing all things into remembrance.
Oh, there's so much that I have learned;
So much good to share with and learn from
My sisters and brothers,
Endless good Jesus teaches me through His word.
And although I don't fully fathom everything,
I want to know more and more each day,
For what an honor it is to be a student
Of the perfect, holy, sovereign God
Who forever reigns.

The baby in my arms

Last night, I had a dream that everything was
Burning to the ground. I ran through the
Smoke-stricken streets, holding a dying
Baby in my arms. I don't know if it was mine,
But I was gravely trying to keep it alive.

I saw myself rushing up the stairs of an
Old tower, baby still in my arms, saying,
"If I just get to the top, you will be fine."
I did make it to the top, and I
Found myself in a crowded room full
Of people in pain and distress. People,
Who like me, thought the same thing—
If I just make it to the top,
My baby will survive.

We were all there to get help,
Covered in ashes, blood, and sweat.
Torn clothes, blistered hands,
A whimper filled with ache,
A cry of rage from those who got
There too late. This waiting room,
I couldn't figure out what it was,
Not even to this day.

I woke up with this heaviness in
My heart; I carried it for the rest
Of the day, wondering if we got
The help we were desperately seeking,
Wondering if the baby in my arms
Made it past that day.

Recently, it seems like there's something
Wrong with the world. But what if it's
Been there all along, and we hadn't
Noticed, never stopped for just a
Moment, and looked, really
Looked at the state of the world,
Really searched for the heart
In humanity?

The heart

How do we keep the fire burning?
Ignite it far more than a small flame?
Surely, we were meant for more
Than just to sit and stare,
Watch the whole world burn,
Not with a metaphorical fire that purifies
But with the one in hell, scorching hot,
Obliterating everything in its way,
Eating at our skin,
But not getting to the root of the problem.

So what if God has been
Offering help all along
And we keep rejecting it?
What if only some were meant to encounter it?

Look, all I know is that in the smoke,
The children of the faith can still see clearly,
While the flock of feces keeps rejecting the truth
And chasing after myths that only lead to damnation;
The perpetual seeking of deathly temptations
Found in the ruins of this world.

The sun also shines

My soul is at peace,
Even though my heart hurts.
My mind feels numb,
But I'm not confused or scared;
I'm not running frantically
Like my past self.
I've now come to enjoy
The simple things in life,
Like milk in my tea
Or the shapely clouds.
So I sit next to my dusty windowsill
As the noisy clock gently drowns out
The rushing cars hoping
To make it to work on time.
The clock smiles at me
Because it knows that time is a
Treasurable asset,
For nobody really knows how much
Of it they have left.
But I just sit here
And watch it slip right out of my hands.

At least that's how others see it—
Like I'm wasting time,
As if I don't make the most out of my days.
But I think I know why I'm no longer
In a constant rush for earthly gains;
I love my Heavenly Father
A little more every day.
Therefore, time doesn't frighten me anymore,
It has lost all control,
It no longer makes sense
In my body, mind, or soul.
And I don't know if that should make me
Happy or sad—
My life is a beautiful, flourishing garden
With an everlasting, melancholic sky.
But don't get me wrong,
The sun also shines
Amongst the gloomy clouds,
And I love it all the same.
I guess that fills me with happiness
On most days, but even then,
I still feel the gravity of this world.
And although I'm at peace,
I have an urgency most wouldn't understand.

Skin & Bones

In the end,
People are not merely
Skin and bones—
They grow tired, not old,
They forget how to live,
Yet they never forget how to love.
My dear, you most certainly
Did not forget how to love.

IDK

I'm in a season of I don't knows—
Where I have so many thoughts and ideas
But it's not a go unless You say so.
And I feel shaken, but I'm choosing
To stand firm—
For although there's uncertainty,
Doubt no longer has room within me.
I will choose Your peace
Every day, through every tear.
And I may not understand what You're doing,
But I trust that it's for my good—
So in every season, my Lord,
I will continue praising You.

For even in my
Unknowingness,
I know You are with me—
You've already worked every detail out,
You've painted my every scene,
You've written my entire story,
And now Your word sings to me
With a mellifluous voice—
Steadying me as I kneel here,
Listening closely,
For even when I don't know,
I know enough to always
Trust and believe.
Whether there be rain, snow,
Or harsh humidity,
May my I don't knows be a blessing,
For I will remain in You,
And You will remain in me—
That's all I need to know
This very minute.

When in my mind I'm a failure

Is Your calling too big for me?
Am I just a small fish
In an ocean of sharks
That only wish to feast?
Will I ever be enough?
Will I ever be bold enough
To speak up?
Will I ever be seen as
Something other than
A young fool whose words
Don't mean much?
Will I ever believe that
I am beautiful enough—
Exactly the way You made me?
For in Your image we were made,
And I know of You to be beautiful,
But why can't I recognize
Beauty in myself?

Letting go of who I think I am
Seems harder than starting over
On most days.
Should I run and hide
In the comfort?
In my timid core?
Where the punches keep coming
And I don't know
If I can withhold
The pain in my mind,
The strife of life,
When You're calling me to
Walk with Your children
Into *unknown* territory
Where a tiny step seems
Like a never-ending leap—
Faith is what we need;
Faith is most definitely what I need.

Father, You've carried me all the way here,
Sustaining every cell in my body
So that I may work tirelessly,
For You are coming as swift as a thief,
And I'm awaiting Your return patiently,
But my heart beats with an avidity far too
Great for words when I think about eternity.
Still, there's so much filth within me
That needs cleaning; there's a dire need for change.
So Father, please clean my heart and change my ways,
And when in my mind I'm a failure,
Can You please remind me
Of what it is that You see in me—
And I hope that it's not too selfish to ask
For such a thing.

P.S. You reminded me that
There's nothing good or special about me,
That You reside in those who believe,
And that I am to be holy
Because You are holy.
That Your grace is more than enough,
That Your Son paid the price
For me on the cross.
And that's truly all I need to know
So that I may destroy
Every questioning day when
I feel like giving up.

And thank You for allowing me
To understand that it was never about me
Or what You saw in me.
For on my own I am not enough,
On my own I am nothing.
I am like trash in the ocean;
A piece of glass being polished
By the tossing and turning of the waves.
At times a painful and unpleasant process,
But necessary for I hope to live
With You in the end.

P.P.S. My Marvelous God,
You are more than enough.
And I can't thank You enough
For all that You've done.
Oh Lord, without You, I am nothing—
We are nothing, and that's
Something the world does *not* want to hear.

My prayer tonight

May You give her grace
And fill her with peace.
At night, no nightmares,
Just lovely dreams.

For I know what it feels like
To be five and terrified
Of the dark, the unseen,
But You have the
Authority over everything.

I pray that You comfort her
And put her mind at ease.
Your power is sovereign,
That, we firmly believe,
So we hold on to You
As we pray together
Before we go to sleep.
Please, Father, give her peace,
Lovely dreams,
And may she fear no evil thing.

Just in case

For my children; always love the Lord
With all your heart, mind, and soul

Just in case
You ever think I'll let you down,
Know that there's a hidden key—
Your inheritance
Is buried deep,
Right in front of the Father's feet.

Just in case
You ever want to walk away,
I left a note—
A reminder in the waves,
A grain of sand
For each of your days.

Just in case
You ever feel like your
Love for me is dwindling,
Know that I left a piece of me
In this world—
A mark that forever remains,
The tender whisper of my voice
For you to cherish.

Creatures of habit

My dear Ally
Went down the wrong path
And got addicted to the kind
Of things that will eventually
Cost her way too much;
Breaking the chain is
Her only hope left,
But what little hope is left,
She keeps pushing away.

My precious friend
Went on a trip
And decided to
Never come back again,
He's now a lost boy and
The world is his lonely
Playground, full of discolored
Slides and rusty swings.
He now walks the streets
Of abandonment and fear.

A beautiful girl hates
The way her stomach hangs,
So she wakes up to exercise at 3 am.
What she doesn't understand is
That she doesn't have to punish
Herself to be healthy,
For true health is not found by
Hating oneself to the point
Of starvation.

So how do I teach her
To love herself?
How do I make life
Desirable to someone
Who only seeks
To obliterate?
How can I show compassion
And not hate?

Can my heart handle
Any more breaks?
Am I too sensitive
To the whole world?
This is my cycle,
I half understand.

We're creatures of prey—
Oh, what would it be like
To live in the light,
But we've stayed in the shade,
Tearing each other apart,
Breaking our bones
Just to look back.

And I do not know
Which one is worse,
To do nothing or to feel like
I have to take on
The whole weight of the world.
It may seem simple,
Until you're faced
With a decision to make—

How to march forward
When we've grown roots
In the place we now stand,
Cultivated habits
In a barren land—
We are hungry for a change,
But how can we leave
Our old lives
And produce the fruit
You so graciously deserve?

Blame Game

When you need to point a finger
But can't find someone to blame,
How would it feel to point it at yourself?

Gleam

When she was playing a fool
And her only audience was me,
When she unleashed her darkness
And her only victim was tied
Hands behind her back,
Facing the unseen—
When she told her best friend
All she ever wanted was to be happy,
When she pretended to be a
Villain but gave in for love and peace,
When she stopped acting like a hero
And realized that she needed healing,
When she finally traded her sorrow for joy,
A miraculous light gleamed—
Now, her story will have a sunny ending.

a "kingdom"

I now understand.
You built your "kingdom" on injustices,
Oh, the mighty fall you fear.
The dearest rivers tainted red,
Where your "love" was spilled,
Corruption prevailed.

I heard them say—
Growing up will mold you
Into a villain.
I said, or are most doomed
From the first day?
You know,
Only a few have been given
Life over death,
Now that I'm older,
I'm trying to comprehend—

Why is it so attractive
To drive the wrong way on the freeway,
Stomp on people's heads,
Lock kids in a cage,
Kill for power,
Wield such power till it leads
You to your own death?

I heard them say—
It's all for true love.
I said, well I think you're
Having an affair.
Your "undivided loyalty"
Contradicts itself,
And I will never fully comprehend
How one can disguise death as life,
For it's crystal clear,
As unmistakable as night and day.
But oh, how I constantly weep
For the fate of those who fall for it.

Look,
I know I'm no better—
I've pressed the "blade"
Against my tongue,
The "gun" against my flesh,
But now, I have laid down
My weapons—
I just hope you'll do the same.

Small-town world

If I were to move to a big city
Where the bright lights
Drown out even the
Most dazzling stars,
Would I change my identity,
Or would I always be me?
Would I alter my appearance?
Would I lose my mind?
Would I lose my peace?
I asked myself these questions
Every passing moment,
With every blink-less stare,
Until a new set of questions
Bubbled up in the hot summer air.

How would I think,
How would I live,
How would I dress,
What would I fear,
If I were forever stuck
In a small-town world
With nowhere to go
And everywhere to be?
Because I'm happy
Here at home,
But I also have
A lot of world left to see.
So would staying here affect
Me more than if I were to leave?
Does a puddle want to be part of
A pond or the sea,
Or would it rather evaporate into
The atmosphere and disappear?
I guess I don't know,
I just know that I don't want to
Live with regret and fear.

Afloat

Hazy is on a boat,
And I'm there too.

How do I get off
When surrounded
By water as far
As my eyes can see?

The bitterness of this feeling
Is a distaste to my mouth,
So this is where I'm at—
Encircled by "nice" guys who like to
Fake their interest in the Light.

They ask, "how do you like to spend your nights?"
I say, "asking questions most wouldn't dare to ask."

It tickles my mind—
To know that I know the answer to
Every part of my life.

So why does confusion have me in a frenzy?
Why is there a conflict in my heart
When I know the boat will sail smoothly
Even if the ocean swirls apart?

I have hope,
But as of now,
I'm stuck on this boat—
That is somehow still
Afloat.

Your word is my treasure

Your word is my treasure,
My hope in things unseen.
Is it enough—
To say I trust and believe
If I keep falling for the lies being fed to me?
Is it true faith—
If every time I feel like I'm reaching the top,
I begin to sink?
Lord, can this be my apology—
Will You please forgive me and
Help me overcome my unbelief?
For Your word is my treasure,
May my life be based solely on
Every phrase I read—
As I tear this tangible book apart by
Studying it endlessly,
Devouring it from beginning to end
Till it becomes a part of me,
Kept inside so that it'll never leave.
Unlike the times I told it to go away,
Then my heart sat heavy from the shame
I carried, sinking a little more day after day.

Lord, I'm sorry for the times
I pushed Your word away from me,
For the times I did not believe,
For the restless nights—
When the predator lurked in all
The places where my mind
Had become weak.
For the days—
When there are no tears left to grief
Because I become so dehydrated
And need Your living word to fill
My every moment. Please.
For Your word is my treasure—
No other written thing will ever be
As valuable to me.
And may nothing in this world
Ever again—
Take the place of You in me,
For You are my treasure;
I now rejoice in knowing that
Heaven is my eternity.

Remember

She would always say,
"It doesn't matter how fast you can glide
Your fingers across the keys or strings,
How high or low you can sing,
How long you can hold the brush before your hand
Goes numb from all the painting,
How bad you think your writing may be,
Or how long before you become better—
But what does better even mean?
Stop comparing yourself, there is beauty
In the minuscule and big,
In the complexity and simplicity,
In your gifting, for it was hand-picked and
Masterfully crafted to be sufficient and unique.
Everything you will ever need,
God gave to you before you could even breathe.
So remember my dear,
It's never about the size of your gift,
It's about what you learn to do with it."

With her words still echoing in my mind, I asked myself—
Will I learn to use my gift to glorify God and no one else?
Will I learn to use it to be the hands and feet of Jesus
So that I may be of some help?
Or will I keep it to myself and bask in the glory?

All those who hate me love death

I don't want to miss a thing. I want to live
In a constant adventure—trusting Jesus
Is all I have left; therefore, I have everything.
I've lived too many years worrying about nothing
And everything all at once. I've run too many
Races that led to discomfort, bitterness,
Folly, and selfish regrets. But somehow
I ended up chasing after Wisdom's tail.
And let me tell you, she's in constant
Motion; you can't outrun her, so that makes
Her the perfect partner to train with,
For no matter how much I pursue,
She keeps pushing me to great new lengths.
She taught me how to love God and not
Worry about what comes next—smiling,
She says, *all those who hate me love death*,
As she springs into her next season,
Unbothered, unscathed.
My mind traces back to the uncontrollable beating
Of my heart, the shaking of my legs;
I knew I wanted to charge after her
The moment we met, but I had to wait
For the right time to become steady and be ready
To walk in her freedom, dance in her rivers,
See the world in colors not known to most men
—Now thanking the Father for the honor and courage
To take Wisdom by the hand as I learn to love Him
And His ways a little more each day,
With the understanding that I must die to my flesh
And abandon the perishable things of this world.

The Mercenary

Hard for her to swallow
Her disdainful sense of self,
Pretentious of her to pretend that she could
Express herself well—
And hoping to be liked and loved
By the rest of the world,
She grew with pride,
Marching on top of everyone
So that she may one day lead the parade,
Wondering what it would be like to shake hands
With money and fame.
She's desirous of peace—
But only within herself,
And found the thought of everyone fading
Like a small puddle quickly
Evaporating on a hot sunny day
Wickedly amusing, not gruesome or strange.

Then her alarm rang,
And so she told herself—
If you keep living in your head,
You'll never go out and see the world,
You'll never find peace,
You'll never care about anyone
But yourself—
You'll never love anything
But the deplorable things that lead
The soul to the grave,
For what good is money if it will
Only lead you to eternal hell?

Hanging by a thread

Sometimes, I feel like I'm hanging by a thread,
And the left side of my head always seems to hurt.
I like to think about my words—
The ones that will never be read,
And how my mind creates such ugly thoughts
That come out in a spurt,
Reminding me of that cruel summer day,
How I almost felt embarrassed,
But then I told myself, this is who I am—
Overthinking is my choice of poison
And my daily dose of Novocain.
So I closed my eyes, and everything I once loved
Became a hologram.
Of course, it wasn't true light;
It was a curse that inflicted pain in my brain,
For I saw my strength leaving,
As I was barely holding on—
Although he's never in a hurry,
He wasn't late to catch me mid-fall.
Then, with all my fears and troubled thoughts
Finally gone,
He said to me, I will always carry you,
So you won't ever have to crawl.
And like a true friend, he was there
Amidst my pain;
I now know that through it all,
Our friendship will remain—
As we seek the Father together in righteousness.

On a lonely Wednesday night

What's left when you work your fingers to the bone—
If all that's visible will one day be gone?
But the unseen will last forever.
So why am I frightened by the terror
Of losing my mind, worrying all the time
About the things I can't control,
Greeting faces—
And never getting to know
What's underneath their skin and how thick their blood is
Because of the years it takes for me to open up.
But today, I'm opening up.

I've been working most of my life—
Scrubbing the mess my mind leaves behind
And gluing the slivers of my heart,
Hoping it'll all make sense someday,
Look back and not regret a single "mistake."
And on a lonely Wednesday night,
Enjoy the hard work my God's fingers brought to life,
For they were never mine, I can't pretend it was I
Who worked with meticulous might.

Unlike those who act like they created the world,
Thinking that by their efforts,
They have been saved and made well.
Oh, what a wrongful way of thinking and living,
How I constantly weep for their fate.

Sadly, they're the ones who accused me of being lazy;
Some even said my mind was a barren land.
But few are those who say—
You've been working far too much,
Find time to rest or go for a walk, stop chasing dollars
And go after the things that truly matter,
Like seeking righteousness or helping a neighbor out.

Eventually, it became clear that some people,
If not most, have a herd mentality.
Therefore, this is the temporary cry of my heart—
Please forgive me if I didn't measure up
To the person you thought I would be,
But I don't want to be another fictitious obscenity;
I'm sick of the made-up characters this world has conceived.
You see, I knew ostracization, berating, and judgement
Were all part of this path,
But I wouldn't change it for no amount—
I have learned to endure through the good and the bad.

Nevertheless, the loneliness
Makes me shiver at night,
And my fingers tremble
At the thought of not working enough.
But will I ever feel enough?

Homesick

I came to the realization
That I'm not lonely—
I'm just extremely homesick
For a home I've yet not seen
But have heard about
My entire life—
And I'll keep seeking it out
Till the day I die,
For I now know it's not a
Human connection I need—
This feeling is otherworldly,
Mysteriously comfortable,
So far away, yet so near.

June knows

My heart beats. Sixty beats per minute, to be exact.
In tune with the ticking of the booming clock on my wall.
At times trying to accelerate in hopes of keeping up
With my mind. My mind—going about nine or ten times
Faster than the tiny water droplets slowly falling from the sky.

But suddenly, the sky decides it's time to let it all out.
So it roars a mighty roar, waging war on everything
That cannot stay dry. My dusty window telling me
Of the inexplicable plight, for it's fiercely being kissed
Against its will, finding no delight.
And my newly planted cactus begins to crave the sunlight,
Growing sicker and sicker of the grey skies
That have been with me for too long.

As for me, I sit motionless, letting
The dread fill my mind because June knows
So much that I do not. She's a seafarer,
But I only know how to travel by land.
So I ask her which one is safer—and I don't get a reply.

I know that she knows that there's so much more
Than what meets the eye.
Therefore, hoping it'll stay afloat, I jump on the boat
Because June seems trustworthy enough for me
To take a leap of faith and embark on a voyage.

I just hope this isn't my greatest tragedy.
It isn't like me to trust easily, but if I don't go,
June will know, and everything I've worked for
Will be lost and forgotten.

Or perhaps the storm will dwindle—
And my heart will somehow become more like my Father's.
Or maybe I'll learn to endure the rumbling raindrops
So that my mind can become strong
Like the calluses on my feet, like the wood this
Boat is made out of, like the fortress that guards my soul;
Every day a little more and more—like the Lord.

Somewhere on the Holloway

She sits there, looking up at the trees
In the middle of a narrow, deserted road,
Remembering how her father used to tell her to hold his hand
As they crossed the bustling streets,
So out of place in the big city, so afraid and meek.
Oh, who would've thought
That her life would drastically change—
From inaudible words to whistling with the birds.
Without a care, freely running barefoot in the golden glare,
Dancing with the melodious rain,
Twirling in the sunken path,
The earthly creatures watching and cheering her on.

It makes her father's heart proud
To know that she grew up so fully known and fully loved,
Never leaving the path that leads the chosen soul
To the heavenly homeland,
For in it is her protection, her divine intervention.

And she says, *I am safe here, amongst the greenery.*
Oh, how it reminds me of my true home.
On earth, I will never belong,
But this is the closest thing to the peaceful garden that
My mind likes to paint—and my heart longs to see.

So she sat there, looking at the hills from afar,
Resting in the Spirit's presence,
Smiling with tears in her eyes,
Patiently waiting for the perfect time,
All the while remembering the words of her father—

Darling, never stray away from the sunken path,
No matter how tempting the higher ground.
That ground will only lead you to a perpetual cycle
Of terrible sin; it will steal your joy and leave you
Broken and overwhelmed—utterly in despair.
But here, you are dearly loved and forever safe.
Therefore, my child, there's no need to get lost
In the dishonorable things found in this world.

Tragic Tragedies

I've heard of writers
Who had a tragic death
A tragic life
A tragic day

I pray
That it not be me
To blink too fast
And miss everything

For even in the
Midst of tragedy
Life triumphs
Over death

So that I may have
Peace over fear
Hope over despair
Care over carelessness

With the knowledge
That an eternity awaits
For all of my days
While I wait

To outlive
My short-lived days
Left on this
Crooked earth

Little Doves

Peace be with you, my dear friends.
I love you all, even if we haven't yet met.
May God's grace rest upon you;
May He give you abounding love and faith.
Be persistent and stay alert,
Love your neighbor
Like yourself,
And love God above all else.
Be kind to strangers,
Be kind to family and friends.
Be giving and fruitful,
Be thoughtful in your words.
Practice unity, practice love.
Pray for wisdom, pray for peace,
And be a helping hand to those in need.
Sing harmoniously, walk steadily.
Be a light amongst the darkness,
And always seek righteousness.
Don't covet, don't steal,
Don't lie, don't kill.
Be pure of mind, body, and soul,
And have a heart that aches to
Right the wrongs.

Find joy in community,
Find joy amid pain.
Practice honesty, compassion, kindness,
And let go of the mindlessness
That leads the soul astray.
Love each other wholeheartedly,
For the word says that love
Covers a multitude of sins.
And don't forget to live, truly live
For Christ, not for this immoral world,
Because the Father has given
His little doves freedom from
Condemnation, abundant grace,
Never-ending love, overwhelming peace,
And an incomparable promise
Of eternity—

Without stain, marveling at His glory,
We will stand before the Mighty King.
Oh Lord, how we love to worship Thee!
But remember my dear friends,
There will be persecution
And slaying because of our faith in Jesus,
For we know that many have already
Lived through it—
Some are currently experiencing it.
So be prepared in season
And out of season; at all times,
For it will be worth it in the end.
We won't ever have to leave
The bliss, the serenity.
The rivers will flow steadily,
Our gardens will bloom eternally,
This dry land will be gone,
Erased from our memory,
And His glory and love will be
All that we know—
Finally fully fathoming
The holiness we now understand
Very little of.

A blooming rose in His hands

The thorn in my flesh
That sometimes keeps me awake
Oh how I bear it
Now
Not yesterday
But now
For it makes me realize
How much I need the Heavenly Father

And that's the loveliest
Realization one could
Ever have

The same old round

The sun comes up and then goes down,
Dancing the same old round.
Yet he never tires or complains
About his duties or his pain.
His frolic is a relentless menace,
For her porcelain skin, a vengeance,
To sun-kissed shoulders a delight,
But a throbbing ache late at night.
And I can't help but wonder
What it'd be like for the sun to be somber,
For he has never known darkness in his time.
Unlike these tripping, sickled feet of mine
That are learning to roam around carefully
Because their soles love the heavenly,
Therefore, tremble at the thought of doing wrong
And seek righteousness their whole life long,
For they are planted on the solid ground,
Nourished by the One who created the same old round.

His blistering brightness almost blinds me,
So I close my eyes and dream of the lonely,
Thinking, the sun shines amongst the dazzling stars
Without comparing the size of each other's scars,
Recognizing that they all have an agonizing story,
Still, none of them deserve even a little bit of glory.
And like a vanishing mist, the loneliness dwindles,
Leaving behind an eerie feeling
That replaces my moldy walls and drenched ceiling,
For in the confinement of my mind
I sometimes feel alone, but I'm not alone;
The rivers of living water flow through
My innermost being, through my bones.
Then everything seems to fade into a fickle memory
As I look up at the sky and miss terribly—
The joyous laughter of the sun,
For the moon's turn has just begun.
But I know he'll rise, as he always does,
Because what will be, already once was.
So dear sun, keep dancing the same old round;
I know many will never grow tired or frown—
At the thought of seeing you again and aiding your pain,
For your Creator has been incredibly kind,
And your light is not in vain.

My mind has found comfort

I can now say—
My mind is a comfortable place.
I like it here;
There's a precious garden
Where thoughts bloom in every color,
Linked to my heart,
The tree branches intertwined with my soul,
As the soles of my feet grow roots
Deeper than the Boscia albitrunca;
The shepherd's tree.
This garden is my very own to keep
Until eternity—
When these brittle bones are
Dead and gone,
I will finally live in heavenly peace.
Until then, may my mind, heart, and soul be
A beautiful thing,
May my days be full of prayer,
And my nights full of restful sleep,
For I can now say—
I have found comfort here.

On the other side of the door

A letter to my past self—
(These were times when I used to scream,
"Lord, I do believe, but help my unbelief")

The door is open, you will walk through it;
Everything He has planned for you
Is on the other side of fear, my dear.
So please trust Him, sleeping on the cold ground
Is not an eternal thing;
Although the night may feel long,
He has given you peace.
And you've always known this.

When you hung grey curtains to
Cover your brightly lit windows
And they perfectly matched the pillows on your wobbly bed,
It wasn't a coincidence; you were aware that the lack of color
Represented the crumbling state of your brain.
You were living in shadows, surrounded by cloudy, ashy skies,
Lifeless, full of trepidation and doubt, tired of feeling
Lost, confused, constantly in mental pain—
Still, you decided to throw several coats of yellow paint
On the once-dull letter that stands on your shelf,
Not falsely hoping for brighter days to come—
Instead, fully confident that they would come.

So you kept fighting, searching for the good,
Endlessly seeking in every corner, trying to find an identity
Because you didn't know who you were
And to whom you belonged—
But He knew you before He formed you
In your mother's womb,
For He had set you apart and loved you
Before you even knew what love was.
Oh child, He has called you out of the darkness into
His marvelous light; don't you think He knows
Where you're headed?
Don't you think He has it all planned out?

Of course, He does.
By His grace, you'll come to an understanding
That your identity is not in the lying mirror
Meekly placed in the corner of your room—
Where your mind crosses from trust to doubt,
The battle becomes harsher, and suddenly,
This war is bloodier than the last.
And you tend to say, *I'm setting my best traps
All over the cold, hard ground—*
But look, now you're stuck in one.

Pushing through the pain,
Mustering just enough strength to drag
Yourself across the floor,
Finally fully aware that true life
Is on the other side of the door.
For the curtain has been broken, and the door remains open
So that every day, His children can make it through,
And soon you will too, for He is the Truth.
Therefore, my dear, put your hope in Him and nothing else,
For He has made a way; He knew it was an impossibility
For you to save yourself with your own thoughts and strength.
So those He has chosen have been redeemed and saved
By the free gift of grace.

Don't you remember that He crafted your story—
Ergo, He know how it ends?
Don't you remember that He said He would be with you
All of your days? So come to Him, and He will give you rest,
For His yoke is easy, His burden is light, and He will be
Your guide through every valley, hill, or bend.
Remember, there's nothing that can come between,
There's nothing that can stop what lies ahead.
You are His child, sin no more and don't ever doubt again,
For the Holy Spirit is guiding you, showing you the way—
And amidst your tribulations, nevertheless, the Father says,
I AM WHO I AM.

In the wilderness

One day, my heart heard the call to a certain kind of
Wilderness this world doesn't seem to understand;
It was the Father graciously calling me
To come into His kingdom through a narrow door
That was fully open—yet invisible to many.

So I said,
"What an honor it is to have been chosen by the King,
To share His glory and His suffering,
To be able to see things for what they are
And not for what our crumbling nature wants them to be,
To rest on the Solid Rock and not be worried or afraid,
To know that He has completely redeemed us because
He never leaves things undone,
Giving hope to those in great dismay.
To glorify Him, for only He is worthy of all praise,
To believe and rejoice in His goodness because of what
He has done and what lies ahead."

And I have yet to see what's behind heaven's gates,
But I trust and believe in the unseen,
For I'm now fully aware that on the other side of the door,
I have found life and peace.
Nothing can come between You and tiny me.
Oh, Mighty King, You will one day vanish all my suffering;
How I look forward to the very day when, with unveiled eyes,
I'll see You, Lord—and I'll run into Your embrace.

The war inside

4/7/21 12:26am

It starts in the mind
And crawls through the body,
Leaving remnants behind,
There's nowhere to hide,
And the war is won
Or lost there—

In the empty space,
In the barren land,
Where the sea stops
And all that's left is dry sand,
So why am I sinking?

But the war was and forever will be
In favor of the One who already
Won it all.

From the fall of man
To redeeming grace,
We've come so far;
A war can't destroy what's been
Fortified in faith
And abounding love.

So look at what we've traded,
Hell for Heaven,
Sin for righteousness,
Pandemonium for peace,
Broken roads for lovely gold streets.

But on earthly streets, our blood
Has been spilled, and it will continue
To be smeared for the sake of our Savior
—His word permeating every corner
So that the blind may see.

Woeful streets, where at times
I've walked, I've crawled,
Some nights I've had to be carried,
Even still, I have inexplicable joy and peace.

But now I'm running, there's an urgency,
A great need to live only for Christ
And to plant His word like tiny seeds that'll
Hopefully grow into giant sequoia trees.
Therefore, I must persevere because
The race isn't over till He says so.

And all I know is that these *lazybones*
Will not face the great wine press
Of God's wrath that will crush
Bones far too wicked,
Far too gone.

For their blood will run red
Like a raging river
Making its way to its final destination,
And they will never be seen again
By the children of the Light,
For their roads were darkened,
Their minds were blocked,
And in perpetual blindness,
They currently live,
Closed off to the truth
—For the truth is a gift
Only the selected perceive.

You see,
The Good Shepherd calls His sheep,
And His sheep come because
They hear His voice.
Thus, the Lord took away the deafness
And blindness of my heart and led me
To an understanding of the truth that can
Only be found in His word, and I discovered
That, in the truth, the war inside is no more;
Now there's only room for peace
And other godly things
—The Holy Spirit is eradicating
All depravity, insanity, and vanity
Within me. Oh, the many reasons
I am filled with glee.

And because I now sow in tears,
I will reap with joyful shouting,
Rejoicing in Him, for I am His craft,
I am a continual river,
I am a work in progress
—Tirelessly fighting the war outside
Against the evil powers of the air,
With the Holy Spirit residing inside,
For I have learned that the battle
Is not of flesh and blood.

So whether it be with
Fresh wounds or scars,
Full-bellied or empty,
With little or with plenty,
I long to live a life of righteousness
For Him and Him alone,
Knowing that one day
—The war outside will be no more
Because the war inside has been won;
My life I've completely surrendered
To Jesus who died for me on the cross.

So Heavenly Father, may this little sheep
Not grow weary as it waits,
May it trust You through every season,
Come fire, wind, or rain.
I yield to Your will, Lord, have Your way,
For You have rooted me in truth so that
I may bloom in peace—something that very few
Get to experience: a true rarity, a priceless gem.

And like a precious stone that's sought after,
Polished and shaped by the hands of the ocean waves,
Father, You have thoroughly searched
And changed my heart.
So even in the battlegrounds,
As persecution and suffering need inch closer,
My mind, body, and soul firmly believe
That Jesus is the King of kings—Lord of all.

...

Suddenly, the sinking ground disappeared
—With it, all my doubts and fears.
Now my mind knows peace,
For He has given it to me.

These *bones* have been forever changed
Because of my Father's grace;
I've been born again.

Offend me

Offend my mind so that I
Can see things clearly,
With eyes mesmerized for my
Treasure in heaven shines dearly.
And His words cascade
Off the page into firm ground,
Through every inch
Where strong roots are found.
Offend my heart so that I
May know Him more,
Untwist my humanity so that I
Can find what I was created for.
Please tell me what I need to hear,
Not what I want.
And if your honesty were to leave
Me feeling nonchalant,
Then offend my hands and feet
To the point of action
So that I won't sit around
Looking for a distraction.
And in the middle of the ocean,
He will be our island,
Our rescue boat,
The hope beyond the shore,
Where we stand, and where we float.

Born Again

Oh, the precious blood
That ran down the cursed tree—
Of the man who never knew sin
But fully took on the pain,
Yet three days later,
He left the grave—
And has promised that all who
Believe and live in Him will
Have life even after death.
So I joyously proclaim,
I've been born again!
I've been born again!
I've been born again!

John 3:1-21

I have been made alive and
Have received the promise of eternal life;
Why would I ever want to go back
To the things that only offer me death?

Oh the mystery

Yet you do not know what your life will be like tomorrow.
You are just a vapor that appears for a little while
and then vanishes away.
                              James 4:14

We do not know what tomorrow holds,
But even as temporal creatures,
We can hold on to the eternal
And embark on the mystery
Of knowing God today.

And as to what it means to be born again—
All I know is that it's a miraculous work of grace.
His doing, His will, all things too grand for me to
Fully comprehend. I just know that I now believe
Wholeheartedly, with every fiber of my being,
From the tip of my toes to the top of my head.

Thank you to all those who made it this far.

It took me four years to complete this book. I almost gave up several times, but the truth is that we are creatures of habit, and I've made it a habit to persevere and write every day. Except now, there's a different motive behind my writing: to glorify God, to share the Gospel, and to bring awareness of how awful life is without Jesus Christ. I hope these things become more evident in my future work. And I pray and hope that you find life through Him, for He is the only way.

All glory to God, forever and ever, amen.